AIR CAMPING

DON & JULIA DOWNIE

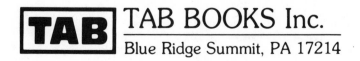

TAB BOOKS Inc.
Blue Ridge Summit, PA 17214

Other TAB Books by the Authors

No. 2280 *Ins and Outs of Ferry Flying*
No. 2208 *Cockpit Navigation Guide (by Don Downie)*
No. 2317 *The Complete Guide to Aeroncas, Citabrias and Decathlons*
No. 2292 *Your Alaskan Flight Plan*
No. 2337 *Your Mexican Flight Plan*
No. 2360 *The Complete Guide to Rutan Aircraft—2nd Edition*

FIRST EDITION

FIRST PRINTING

Copyright © 1985 by TAB BOOKS Inc.

Printed in the United States of America

Library of Congress Cataloging in Publication Data

Downie, Don.
    Air camping.

    Includes index.
    1. Camping—Equipment and supplies.   2. Private
flying.   3. Camp sites, facilities, etc.   4. Airports.
I. Downie, Julia.   II.Title.
GV191.76.D68   1985   688.7'654   84-26904
ISBN 0-8306-2380-9 (pbk.)
Front cover photograph by Don and Julia Downie.

Contents

Introduction

The joys and economies of air camping are known to only a small percentage of today's pilots. With the technical advancements in recent years in the development of lightweight serviceable materials and tasty preserved food products, air camping is better than ever.

We hope this book provides the novice air camper with the background information needed to buy camping equipment compatible with the aircraft at a reasonable cost. There are checklists to assure you take it with you and instructions to make certain it will work in the field. How to load your plane and how to find a suitable flight strip for camping beside your plane are also discussed. Emergency techniques are covered—not to intimidate you, but to provide basic information about the creatures and the elements normally found in the wild.

We share personal experiences while air camping and tell tales of others who enjoy air camping, either solo or in a group. And there are interviews with pilots who carry Hondas in their aircraft. There's also a little on oxygen, pets, survival gear, and photography as they relate to air camping.

If you like to fly, you can't help but like the great outdoors. Air camping is a way to get more enjoyment out of your aircraft.

When we started air camping, we began at ground zero. Neither of use had camped except for occasional family outings or a brief, enforced bivouac in the service. We thought that sleeping bags all came in one size and there were just a couple of kinds of tents.

We thought that a foam mattress might be the world's best sleeping aid—but it didn't fit for us.

Our air camping research was strictly by trial and error. We haunted the backpacking stores. We wasted money on items that didn't work out or were never really needed in the first place. We hauled equipment that was used only once and discarded. (Does anyone want to buy a nearly-new two-burner Coleman stove? How about a slightly used "three-person" tent that wasn't big enough for two large people to sit up in and put their shoes on—much less put two cots in.)

We have found out that many—perhaps most—people old enough to vote really don't want to rough it. We like the capability of comfortable sleeping, good food that isn't a chore to prepare, and other comforts of life—even when far away from home. We've watched other campers and stolen ideas that seemed to work. Now we are quite comfortable camped near our aircraft. If we keep it up long enough, we'll be even more at home away from home.

The procedures and techniques described in this book have worked for us. They may not work for you, so don't attempt to go into any of the areas we've mentioned if they don't fit for you and your aircraft. Go back to the sign on the EAA briefing board for fly-bys at Oshkosh that says: "Don't do nuthin' dumb!"

We gratefully acknowledge the cooperation of *Aero, Private Pilot* and *Western Flyer* for their permission to reprint material originally prepared for their publications.

And a tip of the helmet and goggles to Continental and Lycoming, who have provided the dependable engines for flight over some mighty forlorn country. And our thanks to Cessna for putting fine wings over our heads.

Chapter 1

Why Air Camp?

Air camping can be great, miserable, cold and wet, warm and wonderful, windy and scary, or dull and lots of work—or any combination of the above. When camping, you're subject to the whims of Mother Nature, and sometimes she doesn't fool around. Whatever happens, however, you probably "won't get bored."

As in the Boy Scouts, the air-camper's credo is: "Be Prepared"—for anything! Start out with a worst-case situation and then work backward. Perhaps you want to land on Mile High Meadow and camp under the wing to fish on Troutfull Creek. You already know that there's a camping area with tables and potties, so everything should be great. What's your worst-case situation? That little ol' front that was barely visible on the TV weather report last night suddenly changes its mind and the bottom falls out of the clouds after you've arrived. It's wet and windy, full of IFR with no way to file and, brother, you're going to stay right where you are! For how long? Maybe an extra night, perhaps two or even three before the weather breaks. Be prepared with plenty of food, water, fuel, and other essentials to go with your instant tent, featherweight cots, and sentimental sleeping bags (Fig. 1-1).

If you're among the majority of the pleasure flying population that prefers a good, air-conditioned motel with screens on the windows, warm showers, perhaps a TV to check weather before bedtime, and a good restaurant/bar adjoining, read on.

Perhaps you've become blasé and want to try something new.

1

Fig. 1-1. Camping in an isolated meadow in Idaho is a great way to get away from it all. Wallace and Joyce Bertram have camped with this 1939 Bellanca 14-19 for over 25 years. (Courtesy Joyce Bertram)

Maybe the motels cut too deeply into the travel budget, or the time from wakeup to breakfast to the ride to the airport to finally sagging into the air with a thousand or more miles on the travel agenda for the day has started you thinking about alternatives. Why not save time and perhaps a little money by camping out beside your airplane, ready to launch not too long after daylight into a predominantly dead-calm sky? (High winds and thunderbusters usually are late risers.)

There are almost as many reasons for air camping as there are people who do it. It's just whatever turns you on.

Reason No. 1 might be to get away from it all. Utilize your airplane to travel quickly and easily to the back country. Land at isolated flight strips—within the capabilities of your flying ability and the performance of your aircraft—and hope that you're far enough away from the ground-bound travelers to really enjoy the great out-of-door (Figs. 1-2, 1-3).

Reason No. 2 might be purely economics. As this book is written, a good motel can cost you $50 to $100 per night, and the rates are not coming down. For that, you can pump many gallons of fuel into your plane's tank by staying under the wing for a night or two. Add the intangibles of a night at a motel: cab fare to and from the airport if you can't find a hostelry with a courtesy car; tips; the possibility of expensive bar tabs and dinners, and transportation

Fig. 1-2. Bill Diehl, who manufactures the Arctic Tern aircraft in Anchorage, Alaska, prepares to fish from an isolated sandbar nearly 100 miles northwest of Anchorage. Diehl always carries at least minimal camping equipment including a sleeping bag. Note oversized "tundra tires" for off-airport landings.

Fig. 1-3. A long way from the bright lights, a Maule approaches to land at Quinhagak in western Alaska. George Pappas of Anchorage watches the landing from the shelter of his comfortable pop tent.

back to the airport. Even if the transportation is gratis, it frequently goes with more expensive motels and the cab fare could have been cheaper in the long run.

Reason No. 3 is the saving of time. By the time you unload your baggage and find a cab or courtesy car, you could have your tent out and erected. If you're on a vacation, time is not supposed to be a problem, but most pilots want to get to their eventual destination with a minimum of delay and then spend the time fishing, hunting, goofing off, or whatever. Consider what it costs you in time alone at the motel in the morning. There's usually a lineup for breakfast. Then you wait for the tab to be added and check out, find transportation back to the airport, and load your plane. By that time, you would be well on your way if you'd camped. We usually figure that by the time you're sitting down to the motel's breakfast, you could be airborne in that good, clear, calm early morning air. It is easy to save at least two hours—sometimes much more—by camping out for the evening, getting up at the crack of dawn, brewing coffee and perhaps a little breakfast. You can be in the air by the time you'd still be standing in line at the hotel coffee shop. Then plan a first stop where you can get a meal and go on your way again before the vacation-time weather gets so hot and bumpy that it's a chore.

Reason No. 4 could be the intangible, personal satisfaction of being able to make yourself comfortable in a completely foreign environment. This is always a challenge, though sometimes a minor one once you have the various glitches behind you. How else could a father and his two sons arrive in the isolation of the Liard River on the Alaska Highway and write as follows:

"One of its virtues was that it seemed to be completely isolated from any civilization: There were no buildings anywhere nearby except an abandoned cabin and lookout tower on the strip. In fact, to this day we wonder what useful service it performed. Though the area was uninhabited, its mosquito population more than compensated for this lack. They were so thick that one had to be careful even in breathing. The ground was covered with ripe, wild strawberries."

Reason No. 5 is just the opposite of flying to the end of the map to get away from it all. If you enjoy airplanes and fly-ins, camping on the airport can put you right in the middle where all the action is. We've used our tent, cots, and sleeping bags on the airport at Watsonville, California, for example, while covering the annual antique fly-in for an aviation publication. Here you have a central location, front row center. You eliminate a cab trip to town twice every day, cut the cost of a motel (if you could find one on that busy weekend), save a few bucks on meals and refreshments by either cooking yourself or patronizing the many short-order stands that proliferate at fly-ins (Figs. 1-4, 1-5).

When you camp out at an airshow, you sometimes wind up right in the middle of the action—like it or not. At Watsonville, for example, we pitched our tent beside the Cessna in a designated visitor's camping area that was close to the center of the airport just before dark on a dreary, drizzly day. Shortly after first light, we were awakened by the roar of a big round engine on an aircraft making a low pass down the crosswind runway. From inside the tent, the first impression was that we'd pitched our tent right in the middle of the active runway, but that wasn't really true. Smaller engines soon began to bore smaller holes in the damp, hazy sky that was probably Special VFR, so we laid back and tried to guess which engine went with which airplane. A couple headed for the flight line for breakfast distinctly said, "I wonder if there's still anyone asleep in those tents?" It was 7:30 A.M., and the answer

Fig. 1-4. Camping in the middle of the Watsonville, California fly-in, co-author Don Downie checks out a small folding cot with a small pop tent in the background.

5

Fig. 1-5. Orderly rows of parked aircraft line the taxiway at the annual Abbotsford, B. C. Canadian air show. Many of these visitors will camp beside their aircraft.

we heard was, "No way!" (Fig. 1-5).

Why air camp? Perhaps the answer is in all the things we've mentioned. It does get you away from it all. It saves money and makes you feel that perhaps you've beaten the system, even just a little bit. It certainly saves you time on a trip. It presents a challenge of something different where the best solution for you begins in your own mind. And, if you're looking for a front row center seat at any fly-in, then camping on the airport is the only way to go.

Air camping is always a minor adventure, but it is, to say the least, stimulating. We like it and hope that you do, too.

Chapter 2

Air Camping History

Air camping must be nearly as old as the airplane itself. Barnstormers in their Jennys after WWI, living a gypsy existence traveling from whistlestop to small town and giving rides for $2, $5, or whatever the traffic would bear, frequently slept beneath the wings of their old biplanes—not so often for the awareness of the wide open spaces as to have gas money to get to the next town (Fig. 2-1).

Perhaps some of the heritage of air camping goes back to the rutted dirt roads shortly after WWI when Model T Fords were the popular way to travel cross-country and to isolated campsites. For many years, a 1921 Ford "Kampkar" has been on display at Harrah's Automotive Collection in Reno, right in the same exhibition hall where a V-8 Ford-powered Arrow Sport hung from the ceiling. The "Kampkar" had running board racks for supplies and a horizontally opening side to make room for bedding or sleeping bags with a roll-out tarpaulin awning (Fig. 2-2).

PIETENPOL AIR CAMPER

About the time of the Great Depression, Bernie Pietenpol designed and built the first "Air Camper," powered with the economical, readily available Model A Ford engine.

Popularity of the Pietenpol came about in an unusual manner. Bernie designed and built his first Model A-powered monoplane in early 1929. It flew well and two more versions were built. Early the next year, *Modern Mechanix* magazine ran an article that said

Fig. 2-1. Jennies from World War I were some of the first aircraft used in air camping as barnstormers toured the United States selling rides.

Fig. 2-2. 1921 Ford *Kampkar* was the surface "kissing cousin" of the Pietenpol Air Camper that came along in 1929. (Courtesy The Harrah's Automobile Collection, Reno, Nevada)

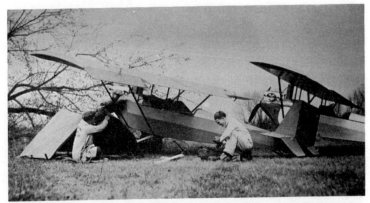

Fig. 2-3. Original Pietenpol Air Camper with Bernie Pietenpol kneeling by the rear of the aircraft. Note simple tent used in this early air camping photo. (Courtesy John Underwood)

automotive engines would never work in airplanes. So Bernie and a friend flew two of the models to St. Paul and invited the editors to look them over. The end result was that Bernie was asked to draw up a set of plans that could be published. The 1932 edition of *Modern Mechanix* "Flying and Glider Manual" carried a full report on what it called the Pietenpol Air Camper and its Model A Ford engine. As a result, hundreds of sets of plans were ordered, probably 1000 in all, before Pietenpol's death in 1984. Latest available FAA records indicate 109 are active, powered with a variety of powerplants. There is an International Pietenpol Association (P.O. Box 127, Blakesburg, IA 52536). (Figs. 2-3, 2-4).

Fig. 2-4. Modern day Pietenpol Air Camper built and flown by Larry Cowell of Tucson, Arizona, at an EAA fly-in at Eloy, Arizona.

Larry Cowell, one of the Pietenpol builders from Tucson, Arizona, advises, "The 'Air Camper' is almost a misnomer. There isn't any baggage space, so the only way camping equipment can be carried is to place it in the front cockpit and fly solo. That doesn't quite fit my picture of 'camping.' Maybe somebody has built a baggage compartment or an external 'bomb' to carry luggage, but I've never heard of either of these solutions being tried.

"I have flown my Pietenpol to Casa Grande, Arizona, fly-ins on two occasions and slept under the wing using a sleeping bag I had belted into the front cockpit. It was great fun! One time I remember well; the airplane had just been completed and I was parked in among the antiques. All night long I'd wake up every hour or so and poke my head out of my sleeping bag. In the moonlight I could see Melba Beard's Bird biplane, a Beech Staggerwing, a J-3 Cub, and even Kavric's Knight Twister. It was like an unbelievable dream. I was proud to have built the Pietenpol and awed to be in such company.

"I have heard innumerable people claim to have learned to fly in the Pietenpols, most of them illegally," continued Cowell. "One man told me he spent six months in the hospital after being outturned by a coyote he was hunting. The coyote got away."

In recent years, the homebuilt Pietenpols have been flown with Corvair engines, smaller Lycoming and Continental aircraft engines, and recently a Canadian conversion of the Ford Fiesta 1600cc engine adapted by Ed Lubitz, Cambridge, Ontario, Canada.

TORTOISE AND HARE

It isn't the speed of the cross-country flying machine that counts. Two airline captains, Jim Ardy and Hector Guzman of Phoenix, Arizona, rebuilt a stock 65-hp J-3 Cub, installed a six-foot-long "Alaskan baggage compartment" aft of the back seat, and took just four days in flying the 70-mph plane from Phoenix to Anchorage where they had no trouble selling it. The pilots would take turns flying during the long summer days while the "passenger" could stretch out in the baggage compartment. Their "tent" was a simple Mylar tarp stretched over a wing and weighted to the ground (Figs. 2-5, 2-6).

WHEN 36 HORSEPOWER WAS ALMOST ENOUGH

Back more years ago than I care to admit, I made my first air camping trip in a C-313, 36-hp, two-cylinder Aeronca K, NC19303.

Fig. 2-5. Airline Captains Hector Guzman, left, and Jim Ardy check their simple camping gear before ferrying the J-3 Cub in the background from Phoenix, Arizona, to Anchorage, Alaska, in four days.

Pasadena, California, embryo pilot Grant McCombs and I shared the cost of $1.00 per hour plus fuel and headed out for a week-long trip from the Los Angeles area to Seattle, Washington, and return. We took out the seat cushions and put in our sleeping bags. Most navigation was done with Standard Oil road maps. A very old logbook shows landings on a ranch near Santa Ynez and an overnight in a stubble field in eastern Oregon near Lapine, where we shared dinner with a Basque sheepherder. Some benevolent force made it possible to pry the 36-hp taildragger out of the meadow and on to Madras, Portland, and Seattle the next day. The camping on this junket was merely that of throwing a sleeping bag under the wing and waking up at daylight. This procedure is great for teenagers, but adults tend to want a bit more comfort.

BAJA BUMMING

Nearly 30 years after the Aeronca K trip, there was a similar experience on a flight to Baja California with Forest Service photographer Tom Roberts in a Piper PA-12. We had Herb Shields, San Dimas, California, as a companion flying solo in his Taylorcraft. This was a four-day bumming-around trip in two slow-and-low taildraggers that could land safely on just about anything. The protection of a two-plane trip made it seem practical to fly into some

11

of the more desolate areas of the Mexican Peninsula that are a calculated risk when you do it alone.

We carried sleeping bags, in-flight snacks, a gallon of water—and that was about it. Meals were obtained at the fish camps along the way at San Felipe and Punta Final. We rolled the sleeping bags in a corner of the porch at Punta Final and then had a fresh fish dinner at the tiny cantina/cafe. Next day it was down the peninsula with the two old taildraggers with stops at Alfoncinas, the mission at San Ignacio, Santa Rosalia and overnight under the wing at the old resort at Punta Chivato just a dozen miles east of Mulege (Fig. 2-7).

With no protection from the sunrise, Roberts and I piled out early, rolled up our sleeping bags and took off for breakfast at Bahia de Los Angeles. Then there was a stop at Alfoncinas and on into Mexicali to clear Mexican Customs. Across the border to Calexico where we cleared U.S. Customs, and then to Brackett Field near Los Angeles—all by 3:00 P.M. The PA-12 is a remarkable airplane for boondocking. It has over six hours of fuel, a big fat wing with slow approach speeds, and good brakes. The almost-two-place back seat is amply wide for another pilot/passenger and a couple of sleep-

Fig. 2-6. Hector Guzman stretches out in the "Alaskan baggage compartment" of the rebuilt J-3 Cub that he and Jim Ardy flew to Alaska. At the time, both were DC-9 captains on Bonanza Airlines in Phoenix, Arizona.

Fig. 2-7. Tom Roberts stretches out beside a Piper PA-12 at Punta Chivato in Baja California. This was a simple "bumming trip" without tents. PA-12 is one of the best back-country airplanes.

ing bags. For the wanderer who is in no great hurry, this is a fine way to go.

It was not until backpacking became popular that adequate, well-designed, lightweight camping equipment became available. Many manufacturers feel that the advent of small economy automobiles helped in this popularity because there just wasn't enough space to accommodate old-fashioned, bulky, heavy camping gear in these new cars. The new tent designs are both weight-saving and relatively economical—ideal for today's air camper. Without such new fabrics and new designs, it is doubtful that air camping would have become as popular as it is today.

Chapter 3

Where to Air Camp

Finding a good place to air camp can be as simple as the next airport or as difficult as following the lure of a flying fish story. Most pilots start their air camping at a field fairly close to home—someplace that they may have visited without camping gear and planned to return. Each local airport will have a selection of fly-out, camp-out spots within a hundred miles or so. Just ask around and you'll find a local place to begin.

Many states have been farsighted in establishing recreational airports. The state of Washington is one of these with 16 airports listed, some of which were originally intended to serve only aircraft in distress. All are classified as "emergency airports." However, they are now used by general aviation aircraft and are located in wonderful recreation areas. The landing fields are also available for forest fire fighting, instructional training and as a base for search and rescue efforts. The state cautions: "Many of these airports are located in rugged terrain and all pilots are cautioned to use them at their own risk. It is strongly recommended that an experienced flier/flight instructor check you out and demonstrate proper techniques before using any of these State airports." (Figs. 3-1, 3-2).

Each of these airports is purported to have or has had both picnic tables and outhouses for campers. A pilot's guide listing each of the state airports is published by the Washington Division of Aeronautics, 8600 Perimeter Road, Boeing Field, Seattle, WA

Fig. 3-1. Bandera State emergency airport as seen from the west. This airport is one of 16 established by Washington state and is open for recreational purposes. Field is 2400 feet long at 1632 feet MSL.

Fig. 3-2. A Piper Arrow modified to a Robertson STOL configuration makes a low pass down the grass strip at Bandera State. Note canyon bottom location and tall trees on the surrounding hillsides. Field may have tall grass and a rough surface.

15

98108. There may be a fee for this booklet to out-of-state pilots.

In our home state of California, many recreational airports with at least tables and outhouses are readily available. Among the most popular are Columbia in the Mother Lode area of the High Sierras and Kern Valley at the north end of Lake Isabella. Here, for a fee of $5 per night, you can taxi into a special tiedown area with running water, fire pits, an outhouse, and tables (Fig. 3-3).

CALIFORNIA'S FIRST STATE RECREATIONAL AIRPORT

The state of California has established a recreational airport at Klammath Glen, just five miles inland from the Pacific Ocean and 23 miles southeast of Crescent City where the airport serves as a fog alternative. The 2400-foot paved airport was opened in late 1978 and we attended the ceremony. A private airport near the new location was built in 1948 by non-pilot S. A. "Andy" McBeth. The first pilot to use this strip was California Congressman Don Clausen (Fig. 3-4, 3-5). During the dedication ceremony, attended by both McBeth and Clausen, the former Congressman told of flying undeveloped motion picture film shot on location nearby for the Lana Turner/Van Heflin movie *Green Dolphin Street* in a WWII surplus BT-13. The present recreational airport was financed with $222,279 (1977 dollars) of state funds from the nonrefundable two-cent tax on general aviation fuel. There are ten tiedown spots.

Fig. 3-3. Kern Valley campground with a paved tiedown area adjoining. Note tables and stove in background. Just 100 yards to the west is the Kern River. Tiedown fee and parking here is $5 per night.

Fig. 3-4. Dedication ceremonies at the California State Klamath Glen Airport southeast of Crescent City. Left to right are former State Director of Aeronautics E. J. McKenney, Congressman Don Clausen, Adriana Gianturco, former Director of CALTRANS, and S. A. "Andy" McBeth, far right, who built the original airport.

Fig. 3-5. Klamath Glen Airport as seen from the air. The Klamath River runs past the left end of the airport. Ten tiedowns are in the foreground.

17

Some of the finest steelhead and salmon fishing in the West can be found at the mouth of the Klammath River, which runs right by the airport. Boat rentals and restaurants are within convenient walking distance of this flight strip. A boat docking ramp is located adjoining the airport on the approach end of Runway 11. Unfortunately, this is the first and so far the only recreational strip to be constructed by the California Department of Transportation.

A number of airports on the eastern side of the High Sierras have grassy plots near their small airport offices that are available for camping. One of these is the town of Independence (Fig. 3-6), where there's a fine Fourth of July fireworks show each year that draws many fly-in visitors. We shared a weekend with the Cessna 170 group, most of whom camped at the airport.

ALASKA: A GREAT GOAL FOR AIR CAMPERS

If your home base is in Florida or the deep South, a camping trip to Canada or Alaska is a long flight. From the West Coast, where we base, it isn't all that far. We've done it ourselves on several occasions and have found the scenery, airports, and facilities outstanding. One of the true experts we met on Alaskan camping is Jim Moody, who works for the State of Alaska Division of Parks in a building within a stone's throw of Lake Hood in Anchorage.

"Describing how we camp up here is like trying to tell someone

Fig. 3-6. A Mooney flies down the east side of the Sierra Nevada mountains south of Independence, California. Many of the small towns in this area permit camping on their airports.

how to walk—it's so routine and natural to us that explaining it to someone else is difficult," said Moody.

"My work with the Division of Parks was aimed mainly at getting better fireplaces, outhouses, and perhaps some picnic tables at a few fields that get a lot of use by local pilots. Personally, I don't even own a tent, although for 25 years up here I've slept under the wing of the plane, beneath a nearby spruce tree, or on the open tundra.

"To attempt to give you a picture of the situation here, with few exceptions Alaskan airports are rudimentary facilities located on the immediate outskirts of the community or settlement they serve. Except at the 20 or 30 largest fields, hangars and passenger terminals are nonexistent. Pilots are generally free to come and go as they please, much as one would use a county road in other states. At some of the larger airports which receive daily or less frequent jet or other scheduled heavy aircraft service, security and compliance with Part 139 of the FARs is of prime concern to the FAA, and we have developed reasonable workable airport operating procedures to satisfy that agency. Hence, other pilots or air travelers must recognize certain regulations or restrictions (Fig. 3-7).

"In general, however, it is my belief that a touring camper, if he observes normal courtesies and customs, will have considerable freedom of movement anywhere in the state. That is, at many small airports he can land and pitch a tent within easy walking distance of his plane."

Fig. 3-7. Picnic and camping area at Northway, Alaska. Shown is a holiday outing by local residents, particularly members of the FAA Flight Service Station seen in the background. Fireplaces are available and overnight camping is encouraged.

19

SPECIAL RULES FOR FOREST SERVICE LAND

A large percentage of our back country is governed by either the U.S. Forest Service or land management by the various states. If you're planning on landing in a park or other designated area, you may need to use permits. Some of these must be obtained in advance; others can be obtained after landing.

Fishing and hunting are authorized under state regulations. Check with the local Ranger before entering areas for fishing or hunting because regulations vary.

The U.S. Department of Agriculture (Forest Service) has extensive rules and regulations for occupancy and use of developed recreation sites. Violation of these regulations can cost you up to $500 or six months imprisonment or both. Violations include failing to dispose of all garbage including paper, cans, bottles, sewage, and waste water. It is illegal to place in or near a stream or lake any substance that may pollute the water. There is a limitation on operating bicycles, motorbikes, or motorcycles on trails not designated for their use. Of course, you are prohibited from cutting timber without a permit and there are restrictions on animals other than seeing-eye dogs. The detailed list is extensive, but it all boils down to judgment and courtesy. If you are in a developed recreation area, check with the local Ranger or pick up U.S.F.S. brochure material before your trip.

AOPA'S AIRPORT DIRECTORY: OUR "WISH BOOK"

One of the best single sources for air camping information is AOPA's annual publication *Airports USA*. This extensive book (636 pages in the 1984 edition) lists at $24.95 for non-members but is available to members free with renewal of membership each year. In our estimation, this single publication is well worth the cost of an AOPA membership. We carry an up-to-date copy in our aircraft at all times, and when we're out cross-country (not necessarily on a camping trip), the book will come open in flight sometime during the afternoon looking for a suitable stop for the night.

The AOPA Directory does not list camping areas separately, but in going through the listings you will find places like Starkville, Oktibbeha, in Mississippi, a 220-foot strip with tourists attractions including a 50-acre lake adjacent to the airport with free fishing to pilots, rental boats, picnic area and camping area adjacent. In Bingham, Maine, for another example, the Gadabout Faddis 2300-foot turf strip has a motor inn and lodge adjacent with camping available. At Cedar Key, Florida, there is camping listed on site at The Cedars, a 2200-foot oiled strip.

When you have time for armchair traveling between trips, a careful look through this AOPA book will show camping spots on or near airports that you've never heard of before (Fig. 3-8).

A number of years ago—1967-69—AOPA published a three-volume series on *Places to Fly*. These books were compilations of travel articles featured in *AOPA Pilot* magazine, many of which were written by us. We covered "Leadville, The Country's Highest Landing Spot," Durango, Colorado, and the high desert of the Southwest. While this series was not prepared specifically for air campers, a large percentage of the areas we photographed and wrote about were suitable for air camping. However, at that time we found very little camping at airports—perhaps because of relatively reasonable motel rates and much less expensive aviation gas, but it is our belief that air camping became a viable, efficient, and increasingly popular way to go only with the advent of modern backpacking equipment. Some outdoor equipment manufacturers and salesmen also attribute the increasing popularity of backpacking campout equipment to the trend toward smaller economy cars. You can't really put a large tent and a two-burner stove, sleeping bags, and ice chest comfortably in the back of the newer small cars.

OF CHARTS AND BROCHURES

Once you've decided on your destination, or if you need help

Fig. 3-8. The Gansner Airport in Quincy, northern California, has a campground and fishing stream adjoining the airport. Field elevation is 3415 feet, making it a popular landing spot during hot days.

in your decision, a look at your set of aeronautical charts—preferably up-to-date ones—is in order. If you are like we are, you'll find the study of these charts before any trip to be a fascinating way to spend an evening. Perhaps you'll discover a new place to stop enroute. Maybe there'll be another campground area near where you're already going.

Don't limit your charts to NOAA's aircraft variety. Go to your local auto club and pick up road maps of your intended route and particularly the area where you want to camp. These surface charts will show roads and trails that are never included on the smaller scale Sectionals. While you're at it, pick up any auto club brochure material on the area, and if you have time in advance, write to the state, county and/or city involved for travel information. These booklets make good preflight reading and also will give your passengers something constructive to do by reading all about the destination while you're enroute.

Many of the State Departments of Aeronautics have for-free charts that include travel tips and background information on many of the tourist attractions. Write in advance and see what you get back. One of the best of these informative charts that we've seen is produced by the British Columbia Aviation Council (#203 438 Agar Drive, International Airport South, Vancouver, B.C., V7B 1A4, Canada).

Many of your best campout areas are out of range of VORs at the lower elevations. If it is your first trip into a given area, a good preflight exercise would be to plot a cross bearing of the nearest two VORs and make your initial approach at a high enough altitude to get you close to the flight strip before you switch over to index-finger-on-the-chart pilotage.

Use of VORs for initial navigation in no way is meant to recommend IFR flight into remote areas. Most of the destinations we mention have no published IFR approach, and a great part of the fun of air camping is eyeballing the scenery on your trip. Even if you and your plane are IFR legal, we'd recommend that you save this part of your flying for city-to-city transportation.

In the back country, ADF is a fine asset, particularly if there is a local commercial band radio station in the vicinity. Low frequency ADF signals can climb hills and drive into valleys that the VHF won't touch. And the new Loran-C sets, we've been told, make it all *very* easy.

As we were completing this book, we had an overnight magazine assignment at the small town of Woodlake at the foot of the High Sierras in Central California. On the charts, the Woodlake Airport is paved and 3200 feet long. It should have been a piece of cake, but we circled for 10 minutes, listening to the traffic reporting on Unicom, before we spotted the strip. It was long overdue for a black seal coat and the string of hangars blended well into the scenery. Always remember that you can see better if the sun is behind you, particularly in haze or smog, so it is frequently advisable to overfly your airport and come back in with the setting sun at your tail.

Being "a little lost" is just like being "a little pregnant."

PRELANDING CHECKOUT

The payoff for all this planning is a comfortable, fully equipped campout. You've done your homework, bought your gear, checked it out, loaded your plane properly, and headed for the great outdoors.

After arriving at your destination airport—hopefully a long grassy strip far from neon signs, freeways, and telephones—you'll circle carefully to get an idea of the airport conditions. There'll be no Unicom in most cases, so give a call in the blind over the field as well as when you decide which way to land.

Many back country airports are obviously one-way strips. Consider the wind conditions and the slope of the runway. Under all but the most extreme conditions, a landing uphill is desirable because you'll have a shorter rollout. Go-arounds on one-way strips can be a problem because of immediately rising terrain,so do it right the first time.

If the grass or sod has been wet recently, look for soft spots as you circle and expect poor braking on the damp surface.

Above all, make certain that the airport is large enough to get back out of comfortably. There are many airplanes that will land over an obstacle, such as a line of trees, in far less distance than they will take off from the same surface (Fig. 3-9).

CHOOSING A TIEDOWN SPOT

So you're safely on the ground and have taxied into your grassy spot. After you deplane, look the area over closely on a first-time visit. Perhaps you'll want to move the ship to another parking area because of high ground,wind breaks, picnic tables, or outhouses. If you have a choice, park your plane in a protected area near the trees. Pick the higher parts of the area to stay out of puddles

Fig. 3-9. Templeton Meadows, a Forest Service strip in the High Sierras of California, was closed by the governing agency as a wilderness area measure. In earlier times, a couple prepare to camp out at Templeton. (Courtesy Don Dwiggins)

when—not *if*—it rains. We always put lightweight aluminum shocks under our wheels and tie the plane down securely. If the wind really comes up, you're going to have enough trouble with your tent and campsite, and the last thing you want to have to do is secure your aircraft.

However, where you park is frequently dictated by designated areas. Some areas just might have prepared tiedown "deadmen" to save you the trouble of using your own gear, but normally you'll have to tether your own machine.

What happens after that—unloading your ship, setting up camp, and getting ready for your stay—will be covered in Chapter 7.

WHERE NOT TO CAMP

If you have chosen private property, flight strip and all, check with the owner/operator before setting up camp. Some areas just don't want visitors. We found this to be true in southern Texas one day, where the fine 4000-foot paved airport and adjoining hangar were reserved by a nearby corporation for its clients' *exclusive* use. Fair enough. We thanked the guard, fired up, and went on our way. Most airports like this are listed in AOPA's Directory as "private, not open to the public."

Some of the isolated resorts where the flight strip is directly associated with the lodge are privately owned and maintained just to serve the paying customers. Unless the lodge is full, you can hardly expect permission to camp out.

In Baja California, Mexico, there are many flight strips that serve just one resort. They take a dim view of air campers unless you can convince the management that you'll patronize the restaurant/bar enough to make it financially advantageous to the proprietor. We have been told that this no-camping-at-the-resort-airport is prevalent in the Bahamas, a destination far from our West Coast that we hope to explore one of these days. Here a private airport can mean "no trespassing," but many are open to visitors. It's best to check in advance. If approval is granted, this should be a super place to air camp.

It's basically a question of using good judgement. If you're not imposing on anyone, taking bucks out of their pockets, or making a nuisance of yourself, most resort operators will give you the green light, even if only for a limited stay.

SUSPECT MARGINAL AIRPORTS

Just because there's a private strip marked on a chart or an airplane parked on the ground doesn't mean that it is an airport. Here are two examples, one that we flew into and perhaps should not have, and the other that we took one look and said, "Thanks, but no thanks."

After we had put a 180-hp Lycoming in the front of the Cessna 170B that we owned for eight years, it was one of the best of the short field airplanes—not technically a STOL, but it would outperform some of the special and expensive STOLs.

We were on a travel magazine assignment on the West Coast and had heard about a resort called Paradise Bar. That's the spot on the Rogue River inland from Gold Beach, Oregon, where the jet boat trips stop for lunch. When it was built, a Super Cub strip was hacked out of a small meadow in back of the resort. We talked with the resort owners by phone before flying in and they cautioned that the field was short—about 1400 feet as we remember it—and the best approach was up the gorge of the Rogue River.

We overflew the area in the afternoon, but hot, windy weather made the area inhospitable. We spent the night at Gold Beach, a colorful spot where camping is permitted adjacent to the airport. Next morning, as soon as the fog had burned off, we headed up the inspiring Rogue River over Agness, where there is a small flight strip, and on up the river. There is a "diamond lane" on the Klammath Falls Sectional Chart, indicating this is a preferred low-level VFR route.

We circled Paradise Bar from a lower altitude, looked at the tiny meadow, and decided to give it a try. The approach down in the midst of the canyon was spectacular. I wish we'd had time to take pictures, but both of us were busy. We came bending around the river, approached the last turn downstream of the resort, dropped flaps, and slowed up. Then we pulled up out of the gorge through a small slot in the trees and landed. There was a little room to spare, but the entire operation was one that required everything to work out *just* right.

While it was quite spectacular, getting out the next day was no problem with the larger engine in the 170B, but we don't plan to fly into that strip again in anything less than a helicopter or perhaps a Turbo Porter. The surroundings are just too marginal for the average conventional four-placer, in our opinion, even with a light load.

IDAHO'S ALLISON RANCH: STIMULATING

A few months later, we had an assignment to write about Harold Thomas, who owns Allison Ranch deep in the heart of Idaho's Salmon River Country. The lead in our printed report started, "If you can land on that 950-foot strip in the bottom of the canyon with your Robertson conversion turbo Cessna 206G, we won't have any trouble with our 180-hp Cessna 170B taildragger."

On the other end of the phone, Thomas, who is also founder, chairman, and chief executive of Trus Joist, gave a chuckle. "That's fine by me. You'll find the strip right at the last bend of the river where it turns southwest. It's about 20 miles upriver from Mackay Bar, and that's on the Sectional. You can't really see my strip until you begin to turn on final approach. Have fun!"

Was it a cinch and did we make it? No, it wasn't—and no, we didn't! We found Mackay Bar easily, all 1900 feet of it (marked as "private" on the Sectional), and then headed up river. We finally found Allison Ranch and located a limp white windsock at the edge of a tiny meadow ringed with trees. So *that* was the flight strip? It didn't look at all inviting and we circled back, dropped half flaps, and flew up the river canyon for a closer look (Fig. 3-10). We soon passed the opening that leads to Allison and it's far too late to start a turn in for landing. We didn't even circle again and found it easy to have a meeting of the minds in the cockpit. It was unanimous to return to Mackay Bar and get hold of Mr. Thomas on the radiotelephone.

While waiting for the resort owner to show up, we talked with Ray Arnold of Cascade, Idaho, who flies boaters on the Salmon

Fig. 3-10. A Cessna departs from the 1900-foot long sod strip at Mackay Bar on the Salmon River. This flight strip serves the adjoining lodge. Prior arrangements would have to be made for air camping.

River with another turbo 206. He flies into Allison on a regular basis and was not too surprised that we had chickened out. When Thomas arrived with the cabin well filled with supplies for the ranch, the two of us climbed aboard and watched the owner do a truly professional job of shoehorning his big 206 into the tiny flight strip at 2500 feet MSL. As he started to turn final, the stall warner was complaining and the Robertson STOL conversion was doing its thing (Figs. 3-11 through 3-18).

That little break in the trees along the bank of "the river of

Fig. 3-11. Deep in the bottom of the Salmon River on base leg to the Allison Ranch flight strip. Aerial pictures of this flight strip were taken from Harold Thomas' STOL Cessna 206.

Fig. 3-12. Turning in on final approach. Note the tiny break in the trees.

no return" quickly opened up into a small meadow where the wind-sock waved lazily. Thomas chopped the power, dropped the 206 on the lip of the gravel runway, sucked up the flaps, and began applying heaving braking. The wall of pine trees at the other end of the strip was intimidating, but then became beautiful as the speed dropped to a walk.

After spending the night in the Thomas' guest house, in what had to be the blackest vista we've ever seen after dark, we watch-

Fig. 3-13. There's the flight strip at Allison Ranch, all 950 feet of it.

Fig. 3-14. White runway end marker and windsock show on short final approach. There is no go-around.

ed the lighting flashes from a thunderstorm and listened to the rain slam against the walls. It really wasn't the best night for a tent. There are no roads, no automobiles, no power lines, and no TV in this rugged isolated area.

The flight out the next day was just as soul-searching. You taxi

Fig. 3-15. Windsock shows right crosswind as Thomas crosses the end of the runway with his STOL 206.

Fig. 3-16. On a subsequent flight by the resort owner, Julia caught the action just a moment before touchdown.

all the way up to the treeline and start rolling down toward the meadow. From there on, there's no "go/no-go point." As we entered the slot in the trees, Thomas hauled back on the wheel and the big 206 staggered into the air. Then came an immediate right turn downstream and we picked up both speed and a little altitude down near the river bottom.

Fig. 3-17. Cargo comes out of the 206 into a small corral to keep livestock away from the parked aircraft. Very old Fordson tractor is used to maintain the flight strip.

Fig. 3-18. Thomas makes a full performance STOL takeoff with no load on board for picture-taking purposes.

By comparison, Mackay Bar looked like downtown as Thomas dropped us off to pick up our 170B. While the flight strips like the two we visited in Idaho are primarily for paying guests, you'll find some of the country's best camping in this area. One of the better fields nearby is the USFS 3500-foot turf strip, elevation 5783 feet, at Big Creek where there is both an adjoining lodge and a USFS campground. AOPA's Directory advises, "Land 18, takeoff 36. Pattern east of the field. Transmit intentions on 122.9. Tiedowns are available."

So there's absolutely nothing wrong in passing up a marginal airport, no matter how big it is, in favor of a field that looks 100 percent safe to you. It goes without saying that a wreck at an isolated airport means that help may be a long way off, and getting your bent bird out would be an expensive trip by helicopter. When in doubt, go elsewhere.

The opportunities for air camping sites are almost endless. As you become more comfortable camping beside your aircraft, you'll keep an eye peeled for new places to visit. Sometimes you'll pass over an interesting spot when you're already at altitude and with a good destination in mind. Mark it on your chart and find out what you can before traveling that way again. Perhaps it will become your best-yet campsite.

Chapter 4

Checklists
Checklists, Checklists,

"We use a checklist," was the comment heard repeatedly while we were gathering material for this book. However, further discussion revealed that the checklist might have been prepared at the last minute from memory or might have been compiled over the last few days prior to the outing. Most commented that they really should save their lists from each trip and use them as a starting place for next time, but they always forgot. We've been keeping our packing lists in a folder for future reference—not only for camping trips, but also for airline travel and cross-country in the four-placer using motels, and this system really works.

Getting that list compiled is the "fun part." If you've never camped, it was suggested by all that you find someone who has and spend a few hours listening and taking notes on suggestions. Most people, however, have had some experience at camping through scouting, family outings, or an overnight trip to the backyard. But even with no ventures whatsoever into this type of life, one thinks of shelter (tent), sleeping (sleeping bags), and eating (stove, plates, food, etc.). So the list-making process is begun (Fig. 4-1).

We break our lists into categories for convenience and to provide multiple applications for different lengths and purposes of trips. We'll share our thinking with you and present some sample listings from which you can prepare your own lists.

Fig. 4-1. Here's the end result of a list for a group flight to Alaska. Jim Smith of Freebird Tours inspects some of the camping gear collected for their summer trip.

PREPARE THE AIRCRAFT

The following list should be very familiar—aircraft documents:

☐ Aircraft Registration Form.
☐ Aircraft Operations Manual.
☐ Airframe and engine logbooks, if applicable.
☐ Preflight checklist.
☐ Radio permit for aircraft.
☐ Appropriate charts (discussed in Chapter 3).

We also like to keep a short list of items always carried in our airplane:

☐ Water.
☐ Portable oxygen (discussed in Chapter 6).
☐ Survival packet (discussed in Chapter 11).
☐ Oil, one quart.
☐ Funnel.
☐ Tiedowns.
☐ Ropes.
☐ Selection of tools.
☐ First aid kit.

AND NOW THE PILOT

- ☐ Pilot's Certificate.
- ☐ Valid physical.
- ☐ Radio telephone permit.
- ☐ Current Bienniel Flight Review endorsement. (Rather than carrying your logbook, we'd suggest having the CFI who gives you your BFR put his stamp on the back of one of his business cards or something similar and sign it; you can carry this right along with your license and medical certificate. This would be in addition to the logbook entry as many insurance companies require the BFR to be "logged.")

IF YOU CROSS THE U.S. BORDER

Some of the best air camping sites in North America are in Canada. Mexico also has a number of good locations (Fig. 4-2). Thus, your trip may become an international one and will require just a little more paper work. While passports are presently not required in either Canada or Mexico, we'd recommend that you carry them anytime you go out of the U.S. It makes it so much easier to get back in!

Whichever international border you cross, remember that it is the pilot's responsibility to take care of all flight plan details and formalities. Make certain you have current information because the potential for stiff fines is always there. U.S. Customs provides a

Fig. 4-2. Simple overnight tent is erected under the wing of a Cessna at the first annual fly-in of the Cardinal Club at Lake Geneva, Wisconsin. Note identical type aircraft lined up in the grass beside the runway.

free booklet, *U.S. Customs Guide for Private Fliers.* This 42-page booklet can be obtained by writing the Department of the Treasury, U.S. Customs, Washington, D. C. 20229.

To cross the border, each person will need proof of citizenship (passport, certified copy of birth certificate, military discharge papers, naturalization papers, etc.) The pilot will need also to present current airman and medical certificates, personal radio telephone license, and notarized permission to use the aircraft if the aircraft is rented, borrowed, or registered in the name of a company, corporation, or partnership.

The only caution for Canada is not to carry a handgun. Rifles or shotguns are permitted; they are *required* for flight over sparsely populated areas. Gun permits for Mexico should be arranged for in advance.

Flight into Mexico requires special aviation insurance coverage for damages to third parties on the ground. Several insurance firms throughout the U.S. are brokers for the Mexican insurance company that provides this required coverage. You must carry proof of this insurance or you will not be permitted to go beyond the airport of entry. We strongly suggest you obtain the coverage before crossing the border, as we have never found anyplace to purchase this insurance at the Mexican international airports and cab trips to town are time consuming and an added expense. We personally find the MexiCard (an insurance credit card) arrangement offered through MacAfee & Edwards insurance agency in Los Angeles, California, very convenient.

PERSONAL ITEMS

The following is a suggested list that again is useful for all travels away from home in your aircraft, always keeping in mind that you can't just pull over at the nearest drugstore along the way and pick up what you forgot:

- ☐ Toothbrush.
- ☐ Toothpaste.
- ☐ Razor.
- ☐ Shaving cream.
- ☐ Soap.
- ☐ Deodorant.
- ☐ Suntan lotion.
- ☐ Insect repellent.
- ☐ Cosmetics.

Fig. 4-3. When you're this far out of civilization, you don't want to run out of personal pharmaceuticals. Julia Downie and George Pappas prepare to fish for salmon in the Nushagak River between Dillingham and King Salmon, Alaska. The amphibious Widgeon owned by Pappas was landed in the river, the gear extended, and then we taxied right up on the beach.

This is a very personal list to be developed in as much detail as individual memories require. We do not recommend, however, that a copy of your eyeglass prescription be carried in your wallet, just in case. And we've found it handy on two occasions to have a record of our prescription medication available with the name and phone number of pharmacy and prescription number. When we ran out, we had the pharmacist in the town we were visiting in Alaska call our pharmacist back home for permission to refill. (Of course, you must make certain that your prescription provides for a refill ahead of time.) The best solution, of course, is to take adequate supplies with you and don't lose them (Fig. 4-3).

DIFFERENT KINDS OF AIR CAMPING

There's no single list that will fit all pilots, their planes, their vacationing destinations, and their personal needs and/or preferences. If you're going camping with a two-place Cessna 140 or 150 and taking a companion, your payload is severely limited and your list will be just about the same as a backpacker (Fig. 4-4). With four people in a four-placer, you're really not that much better off. Serious air campers that we know prefer to take just two people in a four-placer and fill the back end with those items that make your home away from home delightful.

ONE NIGHT STAND

If our only concern in planning our trip is whether or not we'll be able to locate lodgings along the route, or we know ahead of time that we would like to sleep under the wing for time-saving reasons, we only add the tent, cots, and sleeping bags with a small Sterno or primus stove for heating water for coffee in the morning. And, of course, we do need to pack the instant coffee, teaspoon, pan, and two cups. When our plans include camping *per se* along the way, our list gets considerably longer.

FOREST SERVICE RECOMMENDATIONS

While it is designed for backpackers, the USFS has a concise listing of what you should bring for your "wilderness experience." As mentioned previously, the backpacking equipment and concepts match beautifully with air camping because of space and weight considerations (Fig. 4-5). Perhaps you can glean some ideas from the following excerpts from the booklet entitled *Backpacking* (U.S. Department of Agriculture, Forest Service, Program Aid 1239; order from Superintendent of Documents, U.S. Government Printing Office, Washington, D.C. 20402). We picked up a copy at our local Forest Service office.

Fig. 4-4. Camping with a two-place Cessna 152 are David Cleveland and Jane Ross at Costerisan Farms, California. The pop tent, ice chest, chairs, and minimal luggage came in the two-placer.

Fig. 4-5. Backpackers Judy and Wade Dellards leave their Cessna 170 and start a backpacking expedition at Templeton Meadows in the High Sierras. (Courtesy Don Dwiggins)

"Experienced backpackers pride themselves on being able to travel light. Veteran backpackers will seriously explain that they cut towels in half and saw the handles off toothbrushes to save ounces. They measure out just the right amount of food needed and put it in plastic bags, which are light.

"What you need for camping:

- ☐ Tent or tarp for shelter.
- ☐ Sleeping bag.
- ☐ Foam pad.
- ☐ Lightweight stove and fuel.
- ☐ Coated nonstick cooking utensils.
- ☐ Dishes and cutlery.
- ☐ Small flashlight with extra batteries and bulb.
- ☐ Dark glasses.
- ☐ Knife.
- ☐ Waterproof matches.
- ☐ Biodegradable soap.
- ☐ Insect repellent.
- ☐ Litter bags to remove unburnable trash.
- ☐ Compass.

"What you need for clothing:

□ One extra pair of jeans.
□ Long-sleeved cotton shirts.
□ At least two wool shirts.
□ Sweater.
□ Parka or windbreaker.
□ Two changes of wool socks.
□ Underwear.
□ Camp shoes and socks.
□ Rain gear.
□ Handkerchiefs.
□ Hat.

"Using layers of clothing is efficient because it allows for several combinations to meet changing weather conditions. Using clothing in various combinations also reduces the total amount needed on the trip, thus saving weight and space. Wear footwear that is comfortable and appropriate.

"Carry a lightweight shovel or trowel and white toilet papers. Dyed paper may be harmful to the environment.

"Bring maps, towel, water canteen or flask, plastic bags, needle, thread, safety pines, first aid kit and rope (nylon cord).

"Experience will help you refine planning skills, equipment and techniques. However, evenings at home with how-to-do-it books, practice in putting up tents or shelters and trying out dehydrated foods or home recipes will spark the imagination and help you avoid making some mistakes."

CAMPING WITH THE BERTRAMS

One of the best lists we've seen for two people in a small four-placer comes from Joyce and Wallace Bertram of La Canada, California. They have been air camping regularly for more than 25 years in the same 1939 Bellanca 14-19. They supplied us with a recommended "where-to-start" checklist. Wallace Bertram was a U.S. Navy mechanic during WWII, has an A&P rating, and used his expertise to develop the sophisticated tooling required to mass-produce lawn furniture and camping equipment fabricated from aluminum tubing (Fig. 4-6). His wholesale backpacking and camping supply company, Stansport, is one of the nation's larger users of aluminum turbine, buying a quarter of a million feet at a time to supply a single month's production. Both Joyce and "Bert" think backpacking equipment is synonymous with air camping equipment because of the mutuals concerns regarding weight and bulk. They should know, and here's the list they provided:

- [ ] Backpacking tent.
- [ ] Space blankets.
- [ ] Sleeping bags.
- [ ] Lightweight cots (some people carry foam pads or air mattresses only).
- [ ] Foam (Pac-lite) pads with 4-inch foam pads for pillows.
- [ ] Aluminum stools or fold-up aluminum director's chairs.
- [ ] Insect repellent (the Bertrams and the authors use Cutters lotion).
- [ ] Two or three 2-pound coffee cans with plastic lids to be used as cooking utensils.
- [ ] Pair of pliers to do double duty as handle for the coffee cans.
- [ ] Griddle, spatula, large spoon, large fork, and collapsible grill.

Fig. 4-6. Wallace Bertram uses this aluminum tube bender to form the legs of a Stansport Cot. The special equipment was made from surplus WWII bomber parts.

- [ ] Small propane lamp.
- [ ] Flashlights.
- [ ] Plastic plates, cups, forks, knives, and spoons.
- [ ] Small plastic basin which serves as a wash basin, salad bowl, etc.
- [ ] Dehydrated or freeze-dried food.
- [ ] Toilet paper.
- [ ] Packet of soap, liquid detergent.
- [ ] Can of peanuts for an appetizer—save the can to catch grease drippings, which can be used in cooking and maintaining the fire; do not pour it out on the ground.
- [ ] Small terrycloth towels.
- [ ] Ax or garden pruning pull saw to cut firewood; the saw is more efficient, but cannot be used to drive tent poles or aircraft tiedowns.
- [ ] Small shovel.
- [ ] Hank of lightweight nylon rope or twine.
- [ ] Rain parkas.
- [ ] Warm jackets.
- [ ] Lawn and leaf plastic bags; these do double-duty as garbage bags and instant rain protection for equipment and luggage.
- [ ] First aid kit (should be in aircraft already).
- [ ] Ronsonol lighter fluid and matches in a waterproof container (35 mm film container makes a good, compact match holder).
- [ ] Small signaling mirror (should be in aircraft already).
- [ ] Deck of playing cards, in case you're socked in.

MINI-LIST FOR SMALLER HOMEBUILTS

George Scott, an early builder of the Rutan VariEze, from Cummin, Georgia, has a very short packing list when he and his wife fly to Oshkosh (Fig. 4-7). Space is at a premium in this efficient, long-range homebuilt, so George packs for sleeping, coffee, and snacks only. Here's what he takes in a 75-pound total for this nine-day campout:

- [ ] Two-man tent with rain fly.
- [ ] Two full-size pillows, blanket, and two sheets.
- [ ] Sterno stove and fuel.
- [ ] Collapsible 1.5-gallon water jug.
- [ ] Tool kit and spare parts.

Fig. 4-7. A portion of the air camping area at the annual Experimental Aircraft Association Fly-In at Oshkosh, Wisconsin. Special areas are maintained for homebuilts, classics and modern production aircraft. Photo was taken from an EAA helicopter.

- ☐ Sponge, rags, wax.
- ☐ Coffeepot; coffee and tea.
- ☐ Two thermo cups.
- ☐ Clothes for nine days for two.
- ☐ Sectionals and Flight Guide.
- ☐ First aid kit.
- ☐ Snacks and juice.
- ☐ Two folding seats.
- ☐ Two cameras plus film.

ALL BUT THE KITCHEN SINK

J. R. and Yvonne Smith of Los Angeles, California, promote group flying with their Freebird Tours. The list they recommended for participants on the 1984 trips to Alaska is very extensive and thought-provoking. The group tour to Alaska does include a couple camping days. We quote from their handout material and reproduce the 89-item list with the Smiths' permission. You will

Fig. 4-8. Jim and Yvonne Smith set up their camping gear in the backyard before starting on a Freebird Tours trip to Alaska.

note duplication among all the lists we have presented. In Chapter 5, there is more about the items on the Freebird Tours' camping list and more about their trip in Chapter 10 (Figs. 4-8, 4-9).

Must-Have List

Plane-Related Items

☐ Small tool kit.
☐ Tiedowns and extra rope.

Fig. 4-9. Aircraft from Freebird Tours are shown parked in the grass at Watson Lake, Yukon Territory, Canada, on a group flight to Alaska. (Courtesy Jacquelyn Lanpher-Neumann)

- ☐ Oil.
- ☐ Wheel chocks.
- ☐ Survival kit.
- ☐ AOPA trip kit and maps.

Camping Equipment
- ☐ Tent.
- ☐ Sleeping bags.
- ☐ Stove.
- ☐ Food.
- ☐ Camp equipment.
- ☐ Folding shovel.
- ☐ First aid kit.
- ☐ Mosquito headnets.
- ☐ Bug repellent.
- ☐ Porta-potty.

"We would like to point out that while our "Must-Have" list regarding camping equipment may seem strictly related to our campouts, such is not the case," wrote the Smiths. "Every item listed, with the exception of the Porta-potty should, in our opinion, accompany every Alaska-bound pilot for safety's sake! We have flown this area often and have included these items in our packing list whether we intended to camp or not."

Suggested Packing List

"While our suggested packing list may seem somewhat extensive, we have found that with proper packing techniques, all of these items can readily be stored and carried comfortably. While some items may seem trivial, others may seem to indicate overpreparedness.

"Well, we've learned the hard way the trivial items are not so trivial when you don't have them, and to prepare for the worst situation and work backwards. While preparing for any trip, again we suggest that you alone are the best judge of what items you will need to include."

- ☐ Fishing gear.
- ☐ Waders.
- ☐ Hat.
- ☐ Tarp.

- ☐ One raincoat.
- ☐ One pair rubber boots about 12″ high.
- ☐ Camera bags.
- ☐ Umbrella.
- ☐ Disposable lighters and waterproof matches.
- ☐ Towel and washcloth—one each.
- ☐ Robe and thongs.
- ☐ Light clothing.
- ☐ Baggage tags.
- ☐ Flight bag.
- ☐ 30″ long soft duffel per person.
- ☐ One heavy, warm coat.
- ☐ One medium-weight coat.
- ☐ Two warm sweatshirts.
- ☐ One pair thermal underwear.
- ☐ Three wool or heavy cotton button-up shirts.
- ☐ Three pair heavy wool or cotton socks.
- ☐ Five pair jeans.
- ☐ One pair tennis or jogging shoes.
- ☐ Warm vest.
- ☐ Scarf.
- ☐ Gloves.
- ☐ Mosquito headnet.
- ☐ Clothes.
- ☐ Nice outfit for going out.
- ☐ Dried soup.
- ☐ Instant cocoa.
- ☐ Vitamin pills.
- ☐ Aspirin
- ☐ Candy bars and dried snacks.
- ☐ Bar soap.
- ☐ Bug spray.
- ☐ Pam.
- ☐ Antacids.
- ☐ Sugar, instant coffee, creamer, Tang.
- ☐ Liquid soap.
- ☐ Musk oil.
- ☐ Toiletries.
- ☐ Camera.
- ☐ Coffeepot.
- ☐ Travel diary.
- ☐ Playing cards.

- ☐ Binoculars.
- ☐ Portable radio.
- ☐ Padlock.
- ☐ Fishing license.
- ☐ Papers for plane.
- ☐ Pocketknife.
- ☐ Air mattress.
- ☐ Camp stools.
- ☐ Ice chest.
- ☐ Water container.
- ☐ Canteen.
- ☐ Axe.
- ☐ Tent stakes.
- ☐ Fuel.
- ☐ Cooking utensils.
- ☐ Forks and knives.
- ☐ Trash bags.
- ☐ Zip lock bags.
- ☐ Duct tape.
- ☐ Electrical tape.
- ☐ Brochures and travel coupons.
- ☐ Sick bags.
- ☐ Paper towels.
- ☐ Flashlight.
- ☐ Facial tissues.
- ☐ Foil packaged munchies.
- ☐ "Jill's John."

NOW YOU'RE ON YOUR OWN

The foregoing lists are provided as a jumping-off place for the new air camper. As you dabble more deeply into this great way to vacation, you'll undoubtedly modify your personal plane lists to fit your airplane and reason for traveling (Fig. 4-10). You'll delete or add items, depending on whether you're going to an arid area, to the mountains, or to a seashore destination. We met up with Terry McHenry of Los Angeles when he was enroute home with his Mooney. We were all weathered in at Boulder City, Nevada. He advised his wife keeps the list of things to bring, but they always take their own pillows, even if they're staying at motels.

As you become an old pro at this business, you may find that the compilation of a list of equipment for each trip might be

Fig. 4-10. Overnight camping can be as simple as this small, lightweight tent and sleeping bag used by Bob Etter, Arizona. This camping gear fits easily in the small baggage compartment of his restored Piper J-3 Cub.

eliminated by putting all your camping gear in your hangar—if you're fortunate enough to have one—or in a special spot in your garage where it will be all in one pile to go back into your airplane next time out. However, if you use this procedure, be sure that you don't pirate items from this stack for a night of camping out via automobile or that your family or friends don't borrow something that doesn't get back in the proper place.

Everyone we talked with confessed the number of items carried on the first few trips got fewer and fewer as they learned about their own camping needs and patterns. The tendency to carry more than needed seems to be universal.

Chapter 5

What You Need
and Where to Find It

What you need to take on a flying campout depends in part on where you're going and the severity of the weather. The lists in Chapter 4 cover a myriad of items that can go along. Whittling down on these lists will depend on you, your aircraft's capabilities, and your destination.

Before you take your edited list and leap off to the neighborhood backpacking store with checkbook in hand, do your homework and you may save some money. Talk with other campers, particularly those who air camp. Inspect their equipment and note how they handle it—both in the plane and where they camp. Read the outdoor magazines for handy hints and study the ads. Look at outfitters' catalogues and check the prices. Attend an outdoors-type exhibit when there's one in your area. Most large towns have at least one big outdoors show and demonstration each spring in the convention center or auditorium.

Pick up auto club publications if you're a member. Material from the Sierra Club may be useful. Forest Service handouts give considerable information.

Before you go out and buy, attempt to borrow camping equipment from friends and try it out for size. It's surprising how much you will learn—particularly about what *not* to do. You can run a trial campout right in your own backyard, but it is much more realistic to load this gear in your plane—or in one you rent—and fly to a nearby airport that has a grassy area. Then unload and camp for the night. You cheat if you go to the nearby restaurant or the corner mini-market. Use the tent and sleeping bags, the stove, food, and water that you brought with you. After all, this should be a learning experience—and it will be!

WE PRACTICE AIR CAMPING NEAR HOME

Our first planned experience at air camping was in preparation for a month-long trip to Alaska. Our previous camping experience had been slight: a couple of days of bivouac in the service many years ago, and a few nights under the stars over the years.

Just as most newcomers, we managed to do almost everything wrong on our first attempt. Fortunately, this was a trial run at an airport near home so we had the opportunity to learn from our miscues with a minimum of crises. We borrowed a tent, air mattresses, and sleeping bags from movie pilot Mike Dewey, who used this equipment on motorcycle trips. Discovery No. 1: Mike Dewey is shorter than we are and we found out the hard way that sleeping bags come in different lengths!

We had called an FBO at the old Lake Elsinore airport before it flooded and arranged to camp out on the grass beside his hangar for a night. We landed with ample daylight to spare and the Chinese fire drill began. We found that Dewey's inverted-V tent (Fig. 5-1) was a problem because the poles were of different lengths and each had to be inserted in a certain place. The air mattresses were the blow-'em-up-by-lung-power type, and we didn't realize how hard we'd blown them until about midnight. Then, getting them deflated

Fig. 5-1. With borrowed tents and sleeping bags, the authors camped out for the night at Lake Elsinore, California. The air mattresses were too hard, the sleeping bags too short, and the stove a monster. They learned a great deal on that practice trip.

Fig. 5-2. How to blow up an old air mattress. Don Downie hunches down in a too-small tent while getting camping equipment set up for the night on a trial run.

in the morning was akin to wrestling a greased pig on a trampoline (Figs. 5-2, 5-3).

We had also taken along a standard Coleman two-burner stove but nothing to set it on. The top of our suitcase was rickety. All in all, our premier exercise in air camping was so bad that we almost gave camping up as a lost cause. Fortunately, we did try again and again.

Fig. 5-3. Julia Downie sits on a small camp stool with no back at Lake Elsinore during an initial test of borrowed camping equipment. Each time you camp, you learn something new.

THE TIME TO BUY ARRIVES

Finally, after you've done your reading homework with catalogues and magazines and talked with others and perhaps made a trial run of your own, it's time to assemble whatever gear you already have and then go shopping for the remainder.

While it is handy, don't try to purchase everything at the first backpacking or outdoorsman store you visit. Shop for the more significant or larger items just as you would for a new or used car, airplane, or appliance. Visit your nearby discount membership outlets; look into the large chain stores such as Sears, Penney's, or Montgomery Ward. Take a "little black book" and jot down specifications, prices, and availability (you don't want a back-ordered item if your trip is planned to start next week).

Your most expensive items will be tent, sleeping bags, and cooking equipment. With these and the following items, remember the old quotation: "Don't skimp on brake jobs, life vests, or parachutes." In the same breath, don't skimp on basic camping equipment.

A TENT IS A MUST

While sleeping under the stars might be the greatest under ideal conditions, most air campers consider that a good tent is right at the top of their camping list. There are specialized tents for some high-winged aircraft that could be very satisfactory. We haven't tried them as the bottom of the wing on our low-slung Cardinal provides stoop room only.

Most campers today seem to prefer dome-type tents, particularly because they can be erected easily on concrete parking surfaces. This is sometimes necessary on your way to your hoped-for grassy strip with its trout-filled stream running alongside.

Since you're not backpacking and an extra pound or two here and there *within reason* won't hurt, we'd suggest getting a larger tent than you might "get by" with. A two-person dome-type tent will measure 54″ × 84″ (4 1/2 feet by 7 feet), which leaves precious little room for anything more than two sleeping bags. Add two pounds to 7 pounds 8 ounces, plus a few dollars, and you'll have 87″ × 100″ (Fig. 5-4).

We grew in tent capacity from a smaller package to "Super Tent," a seven-foot-tall home-away-from-home with 100″ × 125″ of floor space. Actually, it is a Stansport Super Hex Tent with fly; its total weight is 12 pounds. There are 24 identical fiberglass

Fig. 5-4. Complete seven-foot Super Hex Tent comes in a small package. Don Downie prepares to erect the tent at Costerisan Farms, California, during an ultralight fly-in.

tentpoles, which fit together in units of eight each. After assembling the three sets of poles, you slip them into the sewn sections to form a hoop with the last end set into the webbed pocket at the edge of the tent floor (Fig. 5-5).

It's a small wrestling match to make sure that the eight pole units don't come apart (sometimes they do) in the process of assembling your three hoops. By trial and error, coercion and pro-

Fig. 5-5. Erecting Super Hex is not a one-man job, as Downie finds out. However, two people can put up this large pop tent in less than 20 minutes.

fanity, we finally had the thing fully erected. Our initial record was half an hour. Bert Bertram, who distributes these beauties, says that he can do it in 15 minutes without any help—but he's an experienced camper.

In any event, the added size is well worth the extra effort to us. Call it "Super Tent," "Tilt'n Hilton," or whatever, in this case, big is beautiful (Fig. 5-6).

Should you prefer the inverted-V-type mountain tents, don't plan to stand up. Two-person tents are 5' × 7' but only 36" high, while the three-person unit is 6.5'× 6.5'× 4.75.' Weight of the larger units, including nylon water-repellant carrying bag, two three-section aluminum poles, stakes and ropes, zippered snake band and front door screen, rear window with mesh screening, zippered front screen door, and front door flap is only five pounds.

TENT OVER THE WING

There are both commercial and homemade tents that merely go over the wing and are staked down on both edges. The custom made units will have a sleeve that slips over the wingtip and the top of the tent slides all the way to the center section, making it possible to enter the cabin from the back of the tent. These come complete with floor and Velcroed panels for mosquito-proof ventilation (Fig. 5-7).

If your campground is such that you can taxi the airplane right into it, then this system is fine. If the campground is adjacent to

Fig.5-6. Super Hex Tent before the rain fly was installed. Cover over the dome provides protection from both heat and rain.

Fig. 5-7. Custom-made tent fits over the wing of a Skylane. This configuration makes it possible to leave items in the cockpit and reach them without going outside. The main disadvantage is that it will not operate without the airplane as a tent pole, so the adjoining campgrounds can't be used. (Courtesy Raettig Photo Service)

the parking area, you'll have a problem with this type of tent. However, if you can pitch your tent so that any part of the airplane will protect it from the elements as well as provide a fairly secure tiedown post, then take advantage of the layout.

One of the most useful items that should be put on the ground before unfolding your tent is a tarpaulin or large sheet of heavy-duty vinyl to erect your tent over. This will hopefully deter any moisture from coming up from below. A second large tarp, one of the items that the Bertrams recommend, is to drape over the wing of the plane and to a nearby tree—or whatever—to create a protected area outside the tent in case of a prolonged rain. This added area to move around in can cool flaring tempers and save friendships when the rain goes on—and on, and on . . .

FASTEST TENT IN THE WEST

Veteran air campers will try every shortcut in the book to cut down on the work of setting up camp. Duane Binnall has developed his own "fastest tent in the West." He concocted his invention on the sly and was able to win a couple bets with fellow air campers regarding who would have his tent up first. Unbeknownst to his flying/camping friends, Duane altered his pop tent so that he could use six unjointed poles, similar to those seen on the back of bicycles with an identification flag atop them. In fact, the poles were straight from the local bike shop. The poles are fitted permanently into the floor of his pop tent with ample room to spare for packing the back of his Cessna 182 with the back seat out. The six poles are then

Fig. 5-8. Duane Binnall begins erection of his "fastest tent in the West." Fiberglass poles remain inserted in the tent.

fitted into a perforated, circular aluminum disk at the top of the tent (Figs. 5-8 through 5-11).

Then Binnall managed to set up a wager with his friends as to which camper could set up his tent in the shortest period of time. Binnall won hands down after he shook the tent out of its handy-dandy sheath, unrolled the tent with the poles already in place, and erected the dome tent by merely sticking the ends of the six poles into the webbed slot provided—and the job was done.

Fig. 5-9. Small aluminum disk has holes to accept the fiberglass tent poles.

Fig. 5-10. Erecting a pop tent in a wind can be interesting. Here Duane Binnall wrestles with his tent while Peggy folds up the small carrying case used for the tent.

SLEEPING BAGS MAKE THE DIFFERENCE

When it comes to sleeping bags, consider the climate where you plan to camp. It's a waste of money and space to purchase a bag designed for the Arctic winter when you're going to stay in moderate climates. Look at models that are designed for the

Fig. 5-11. Completed pop tent erected in well under two minutes. Back seat of the Cessna 182 is removed for camping equipment and two-piece Honda motorcycle.

temperature range you normally expect. Get one that is fully large enough and in the configuration you prefer. Some people like the mummy bag that tapers toward the feet. Others like the his-and-hers combinations. This again depends on the personality of the couple. We carry bags that are modified mummy shape but also his-and-her compatible in that we can zip them together. However, we have yet to find a two-person-wide mattress arrangement that will fold up easily. And with the cots we presently use, we'll live alone and love it as far as sack time in the camping scene is concerned.

We've never tried this one, but it has been recommended: when buying his-and-hers sleeping bags, consider one of expensive down and the other constructed from manmade fiber. This makes it possible to put the down bag next to the ground when the weather is cold and use the less-warm fiber over the top. In reverse, the fiber compacts less and is a more effective insulator below. Remember that the down bag, while it compacts well, is useless once you get it wet—and it'll take days to dry.

The new self-inflating air mattress may well be the best of two worlds. They are really foam pads covered with an airtight nylon envelope. When you open the valve, the foam expands and air goes into the pad. If that isn't enough, you can breathe into it for a larger inflation. When it comes time to break camp, roll it up with the valve open to purge the system—or so the advertisements say.

TRY TO SIT IN COMFORT

The size of your aircraft and cabin space will also dictate what sort of chairs you take. Sitting on the cold, lumpy ground really isn't the way to go and almost anything is better. The simplest aluminum folding camp stool (16" high, 14" wide) weighs only one pound. A second version, 14" × 14" × 8", has a heavy-duty steel frame and is recommended as "great for backpackers, campers, hunters, and spectators." The trouble for us with both of these simple tools is that there is no backrest. Why not go a step further and sit in complete comfort with a Campa-Chair (folding director's chairs) or something comparable. This unit is dining height, 17" with a back that goes up to 33". It folds to only 2" thick and weighs just 3.5 pounds. Sure, the weight does add up, but that's why so many air campers are just two people in a full four-place airplane.

There are sand chairs with arms that are 18" wide with a back that goes up to 21", but the seat is just 6" off the ground. That's fine for youngsters, but a long way up and down for tall, mature adults (Fig. 5-12).

When choosing a chair, we suggest you don't try to cram an ample posterior onto a stool that's either 8″ or 10″ wide—it does only about half the job. Even the aluminum backyard lawn chairs make ideal resting spots if space permits carrying them. After a day of flying, hiking, or even just loafing, there's nothing like the pure luxury of a backrest compared with a simple stool.

Frank Smith, co-owner of East-Way Products in Ayden, North Carolina, not only dabbles in ultralights but also has developed a "Carry-Ease" chair. These units are made of galvanized steel with nylon seat and back. They fold up into a zippered carrying bag (3″ × 3″ × 19″) and have rubber leg boots. Colors are red, blue, or camouflage and the weight of each unit is about four pounds.

While we're talking about chairs, this is probably as good a place as any to mention a porta-potty. Jim and Yvonne Smith of Freebird Tours strongly recommend carrying one. They have the small folding type with disposable plastic bags. These are lightweight, pack easily, and sell for under $10. "We've used this type for over 15 years and haven't found a better one yet," they advised.

There's even a vinyl shower stall with an outside water bag that will heat to some extent in the sun, producing a more-or-less

Fig. 5-12. Comfortable camp chairs add to the enjoyment of a camp out by the airport. Here Bob Weston cleans up the camp before going fishing at Kern Valley, California. Special parking ramp in the background was built adjoining the camping area.

Fig. 5-13. Yvonne Smith uses a two-burner propane stove with a permanent stand to prepare a chili dinner for a group of Freebird Tours' guests on the airport at Watson Lake, Yukon Territory, Canada. Note lightweight awning that provides sun and rain protection. (Courtesy Jacquelyn Lanpher-Neumann)

warm shower. And then, if you're in a crowded camping area, you can install the porta-potty inside between showers for an added touch of privacy.

HOW MUCH STOVE IS ENOUGH?

Like tents, stoves come in all sizes and shapes. They'll range from tiny backpacker's jewels that weigh ounces and will heat just enough food and water for one to elaborate two and four-burner units designed for the automotive crowd. Even the old standard two-burner Coleman equipped with two propane bottles can be a bit much. We used one of these on our first two air camping efforts, but have since changed to a single-burner, propane-powered Primus stove. We also carry a can of Sterno and small foldable aluminum unit that sets up with the Sterno to make another stove burner available. These may take a little juggling to get a complete hot meal for two with everything coming up at the same time, but the price and the weight are right (Fig. 5-13).

Unfortunately, most gasoline stoves won't operate on high-octane av/gas. They want white gas, and that means carrying an extra container of a flammable liquid. These containers can expand at altitude, break, and spray fuel all over the place. Bottled propane gas for stove and lantern fuel is usually considered best even though the containers add a pound or two of weight. Experts also told us that a can of Sterno burns cooler than propane and therefore takes longer; but we have used it to prepare a simple breakfast.

Two air campers we know recommend carrying a small sack of commercial charcoal, for use either in a small hibachi or dirt pit with a grill over the hole. Av/gas can replace starter fluid. Charcoal makes an inefficient fire, but if you're cooking burgers or steaks, the flavor is great. Besides, it's more picturesque than propane.

ADD A LITTLE LIGHT TO THE SUBJECT

Lighting is usually necessary for the air camper as more times than not we land just at dusk and the darkness usually descends before we're quite finished setting up. So the flashlights and lanterns play an important role. And again, there is a wide variety of styles and types of illumination. For the same reason that you wouldn't select a gasoline stove, you would rule out a gasoline lantern. There are battery lanterns and propane lanterns and each has attendant expenses. As you make your final selections, read the fine print. For example, perhaps that nice little propane lamp that sells for $11.95 doesn't include the bottle of fuel that's attached for display. (The sales clerk fortunately called our attention to that one.) Then we discovered it was difficult to find replace mantles for another lantern, and they cost a dollar each when we finally did. Be sure to check both cost and availability of replacement parts. This, of course, is a good reason to purchase brand-name items.

We have battery-operated lanterns, which we enjoy because they are completely silent during operation and very quick to snap on and off. However, extra batteries are heavy to carry, so we use these when we're going to be away only a night or two and are certain the current batteries will last. We acquired these battery lamps initially for use when the electricity goes out at home; we would not have purchased them just for camping. For the more extensive trips, we use a Primus propane lantern. Our experience has been that the propane bottle lasts a long, long time and the lantern gives off a great deal of illumination, even though it is noisy.

DON'T FORGET THE WATER JUG

There is a collapsible 2 1/2-gallon water carrier made by

Stansport that can be hung on a nearby tree or lift strut. Many times, the water hydrant is at the FBO's office or far removed from your camp. Also, 2 1/2 gallons is about the best size for comfortable toting. We regularly carry at least a gallon of bottled water on all flights out of our local area. Those southwest deserts get hot and lonesome if you have to land. With water, you can survive for a long time.

In addition to the campsite jug, plan to have water accessible in the cockpit in flight. Some of those high-calorie munchies get awfully dry without some cool liquid to wash them down. One of the best water containers we've found is sold in Canada and Alaska. It is a heavy-duty plastic quart container with a solid screw-in lid. Put the container in the freezer a day or so before takeoff on your first leg and you'll have a solid chunk of frozen water to go into a small ice chest (which travels within reach of the pilots in our aircraft). As the ice begins to melt, you have cold drinking water in a handy-sized container. We have found that 48 hours into our trip there is *still* a chunk of ice floating inside that container.

WANTED: AN EFFICIENT AIR CAMPING TABLE

With all the fine, modern camping equipment now available, the one area not addressed is a table suitable for the air camper. We've tried TV trays and found them somewhat better than nothing, but too flimsy to use for the stove. A handy-do-it-yourselfer could probably come up with a heavy-duty, lightweight design that would collapse in some way for fitting into the aircraft easily. After all, if you can cut the traveling Honda in half, a two-part table should be a cinch.

Some campers have tried to use the stabilizer of their plane as a table. This is marginally satisfactory if the plane has a fixed stabilizer, but aircraft such as the Piper Cherokees and our Cardinal have full-tilting stabilators and are useless as tables.

Particular care should be taken to have a secure place on which to set your stove. If you drop that stove, there's always a chance of starting a grass fire, particularly with stoves run on liquid fuel. And in this same vein, when starting your airplane in that grassy meadow, be sure not to overprime and backfire. Backfires can start fires in dry grass and that is the reason three aircraft were lost during a recent fly-in in Southern California.

A LITTLE ON SPACE BLANKETS AND FIREARMS

The super-lightweight, super-reflective space blankets have a variety of uses around your airplane. At the airport, they can shield your instrument panel—or your entire cabin—from the sun's ultraviolet rays and the curious eyes of passersby. We carry two of these panels about six feet square in our Cessna at all times. One is used to protect the instrument panel and hopefully cut down on maintenance for avionics and instruments. The second covers whatever baggage we have aboard.

Space blankets vary in cost from $5 to over $15, but campers report that there is little difference except in the brand name. Perhaps here can you go with the cheapie and not get burned.

Whether or not to carry a gun depends on the temperament of the air camper and his/her destination. Some sort of a rifle is required in Canada and Alaska in certain areas, but handguns (under 14″ barrel) are strictly prohibited in Canada. Along this route, we carry on old single-shot 20-gauge shotgun and it goes underneath everything in packing. The box of shells should go in the glove compartment or some other protected area. Should the trip be for hunting, you would be carrying guns, but the majority of air campers we talked with do not carry a gun. Most campers point out that no animals, except fellow humans, ever give campers a bad time. It is a relatively simple matter to animalproof your camp by putting all food in sealed containers to eliminate inviting odors. There are additional provisions for campers in bear country and if you write to the U.S. Forest Service, you can obtain a pamphlet on the subject. Also, we have included a little more about bears in Chapter 8.

COTS ARE PURE LUXURY

We've tried air mattresses, foam pads, and an extra sleeping bag underneath, but nothing we've used provided the comfort of our most recent acquisition, aluminum cots. Weight is only five pounds and the cots keep your ever-lovin' body up away from the rocks, the packed sand, and the lumps that always seem to appear suddenly in your sleeping area just as you're ready to doze off.

The cots are 6″ long, 25″ wide, and 9″ high. They break down easily into a small package to carry in your baggage compartment. We purchased our set at a discount department store near home, GEMCO, but they are carried in most sporting stores. We used them first at a Watsonville fly-in and had a few learning problems. There is a knack to putting them together the first time, so, as the instructions say, "Make sure that all three legs are bottomed on sockets before using." We hadn't!

Fig. 5-14. It takes a flick of the wrist and a gentle shove with the heel of your hand to seat the legs of the aluminum cots the first time you use them.

Somewhere during the night, Don rolled over and one leg of the new cot came loose. He wasn't able to perform a field repair in the dark and after a few profane moments of pushing and shoving, he gave up and swapped ends with the sleeping bag to let his feet hang toward the low end.

Upon our return, we called GEMCO and were finally directed to Goode Products, Inc., (which are distributed by Stansport) and that's how we first met Wallace (Bert) Bertram. He demonstrated the procedure for properly seating the aluminum legs initially. After that, they go together almost automatically (Fig. 5-14).

"There's a little twist of the wrist that's needed in sliding the cot legs into place. It's something I can't really explain," he said, "it needs to be demonstrated." He showed us how and we've had no trouble since.

These cots come in a number of sizes. For lighter-weight people there's a model that weighs less than ours. For limited space in a cabin area, there's even a double-decker that also can be used as two singles. Try 'em; we're certain you'll like 'em!

So much for suggested items. You'll make you own want-to-buy list for your individual requirements and the elasticity of your pocketbook. The shopping and the planning should be fun. But the payoff comes later at the campsite (Chapter 8).

Chapter 6

Additional
Take-Alongs

There are many items you can take air camping that might not be considered essential. However, if they add to the enjoyment of the trip, make it more comfortable, or perhaps a little safer, they may in fact be personal "necessaries."

PICTURE PERFECT PARAPHERNALIA

One of the best ways to share the enjoyment of your trip is to photograph it for showing to your friends. Today's automatic 35mm cameras will make the most inexperienced duffer into a good photographer. Perhaps we place more emphasis on cameras and film than the average camper because good photos are part and parcel of writing magazine articles and books, giving slide shows, and generally sharing our travels.

Regardless of what camera(s) you take, include them in your preflight check list. Shoot a short roll of film and get it processed. There's nothing worse than a great scenic air shot taken with outdated film or a camera that malfunctioned—and we speak from experience on the malfunctioning.

Everyone has his own favorite camera, but after a lifetime of photography and flying, we'd recommend nothing smaller than a standard 35mm format. In our opinion, the new disk cameras and others that produce miniature-sized negatives seldom result in anything more than mediocre snapshot quality. Recently, a friend who shall remain nameless went along on a four-plane trip for two weeks. The scenery was fabulous, the formation flying outstanding, and the opportunity will not present itself again in the near future. He came back with a stack of fuzzy color prints enlarged from the color negative of a disk camera. We suggest you discuss this with your local camera store.

The new computer-generated zoom lenses are producing some great results. Thus you can have an almost universal camera. Many of the illustrations in this book were taken with a 35mm Canon F1 equipped with a 35mm—200mm f3.5 Tokina AT-X lens. This combination gives an excellent range of focal length. It is heavier than some units, but nowhere nearly as heavy as the 6×7 Pentax that we use for serious air-to-air photos and magazine color illustrations. In all cases, take and use *plenty* of film.

Remember to keep your cameras out of the sun. And for those with automatic exposure meters, do not leave them in the glareshield under the compass. The magnets in exposure meters can do disastrous things to a magnetic compass.

For your scenic shots in flight, try to shoot through an opening in the plexiglass. Many windows are tinted and this will throw your color balance clear out the window. Many of the Cessnas have a complete window that can be opened easily in flight. It's windy and will blow loose papers around, but the resulting photos are great. Some aircraft have storm windows on the pilot's side window. These are frequently hard to reach with a camera, but it's worth the effort. We have an FAA-approved folding camera window on the right cabin door of our Cardinal because the windows do not open. Why the *right* side? Don has been an instructor for many years and is very comfortable in the right seat. By always sitting in the left seat, Julia is able to fly easily and conveniently on air-to-air photography assignments while Don handles the cameras (Fig. 6-1).

One word of caution on taking pictures of your friends in flight enroute to your campsite: Formation flying is not taught except in a few military schools. Learning to "formate" isn't all that easy, so rely on the telephoto lenses and don't try to get *too* friendly in the air. Our voice-activated intercom system is a great help in photo flying because both pilot and photographer have instant communication even if they're almost back-to-back.

Until there is a breakthrough in film stock, you should decide in advance whether you want a photo album or to present projected color slides. Each takes a different type of film, and while a good color lab can make slides out of print film and vice versa, it is time-

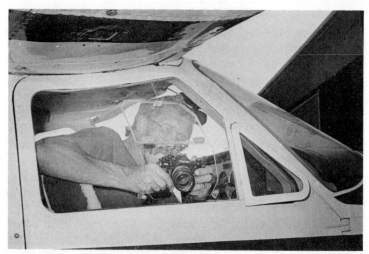

Fig. 6-1. Special camera window used by the authors in their Cardinal. Mechanic Jim Herron, who made the FAA-approved installation, shows how the system works.

consuming and expensive. We shoot mainly 35mm color slides, using a medium 64 speed Eastman Kodachrome film with Eastman processing.

If you prefer color negative film and prints, you will be able to take advantage of the many one-hour photo shops that are springing up nationwide.

Telling a picture story is a personal expression that some consider an art form. Try to take your viewer along for the ride and let him enjoy the scenery, the close-ups of the people you visited, the wildlife (either in the forest or on the beach), and share the sunsets or sunrises. (Personally, we prefer the sunsets as one has to rise early to catch the sunrise!)

In recent years, the cost and complexity of portable videotape cameras has dropped. Now many hobbyists shoot a record of their travels in this manner. Hopefully, this tape will be edited at the conclusion of the trip and only the most interesting sections shown to friends back home.

No matter what media you use, you'll make friends and keep old friends if you edit the slides after the trip. If there's a picture you have to make an excuse for, leave it out!

PETS CAN BE CAMPERS

If you have a pet dog, you may want to bring it along—but

be prepared for a lot of extra work. Cats as a general rule don't travel well, but dogs seem to enjoy small airplanes. Ces and Pam Collings of Christchurch, New Zealand, go camping in their Maule with a 65-pound dog named Sandy. Pam is Investigating Officer for the New Zealand Civil Aviation Division Regional Office in Christchurch. She flies competition aerobatics in a Pitts when time permits.

Pam explains, "We decided that a 65-pound dog would be quite a projectile if a mishap occurred. With that in mind, we made a harness for Sandy which is secured by seat belts" (Fig. 6-2).

"The first trip we made with Sandy, she was a bit nervous for a while and then settled down nicely. We landed on a back country airstrip, which was a bit rough but no problem for the Maule. When we parked and let her out, Sandy was a completely changed animal—lots of open space, hills, trees, rabbits—what a joy for a dog! Sandy now associates the airplane with somewhere to go. Now she is quite settled and is more likely to lie down and go to sleep once we are airborne."

Pam Collings continued talking about camping with Sandy: "We have a small nylon two-man hikers' tent, a bit of a squeeze with Sandy, too. Once in, you don't move or you lose your place. I made the mistake the first night of sitting up to settle Sandy down when she was restless and she promptly moved in and curled up on my pillow!"

Pam and Ces advised that "There is a great scope for landing

Fig. 6-2. Sandy, a 65-pound flying dog from New Zealand, is shown with her special restraining harness, which is hooked to the back seat belt in the Maule to keep the dog from becoming a projectile in case of a mishap. (Courtesy Pam Collings)

Fig. 6-3. Sebastian, a 150-pound St. Bernard, takes up the whole back seat of this Mooney when he flies with Mr. and Mrs. George McCay.

on back country bush airstrips and beaches in the southern area of the South Island of New Zealand. We plan a camping holiday to explore these areas." (We visited New Zealand in 1982-83 and plan to return. This is a country that welcomes pilots and Americans. There are aircraft that can be rented from Aero Clubs after passing a simple written exam on rules and regulations in that island country down under. In our personal wishbook of places to revisit, New Zealand is at the top of the list. Next time there, we'll join Pam and Ces in exploring some of those bush strips.)

DOGS FLY IN ALL SIZES

The largest air travelling dog we've ever seen is Sebastian, a 150-pound St. Bernard that flies all over the country with owners George and Evelyn McCay of McLain, Virginia. We met them on the ramp of the Orlando Airport during an AOPA convention in Florida. According to the owners, the amiable St. Bernard took up the *whole* back seat (Fig. 6-3). If the McCays were ever to camp out with Sebastian along, there would be few unannounced visitors.

At the other end of the spectrum, Manuel Sparks of El Cajon, California, regularly flies with Cheri, a small poodle, in his open-air Pietenpol replica. The dog rides inside the pilot's flying jacket with her head sticking out in the slipstream (Fig. 6-4). Sparks reports that his dog is equally at home when he rides a motorcycle.

Many years ago, we had a mixed breed mutt named Snuffy.

He became part of the family when Dr. Paul MacCready had two young pups that just didn't get along. One thing led to another and Snuffy (a slight nasal impediment was apparent) landed in our household. He was as at home in a plane as in a car. Open the plane's door and he was the first one in. After takeoff, he'd curl up and go to sleep, but as soon as you throttled back for an approach, he was on his hind feet, nose at the window and looking out. Then, as soon as the cabin door opened, he was outside and looking. We never took him camping, but I would surmise that you'd either have to keep him on a leash or you might or might not find him the next morning.

If you plan to camp at a Forest Service strip, there are strict regulations about dogs. Government park regulations state: "Bringing in or possessing an animal, other than a seeing dog, unless it is crated, caged, or under a leash not longer than six feet, or otherwise under physical restraintive control" is prohibited. The Forest Services noted that "Bears and dogs don't mix. It is a good idea to leave your dog at home when you hike or camp, especially in bear country. A dog can easily disturb a bear and lead it back to you."

RUBBER RAFTS FOR FISHING

Many air campers will include a lightweight inflatable raft for

Fig. 6-4. Manuel Sparks shows off Cheri, who usually sits snugly inside Manuel's jacket when he flies his 85-hp Pietenpol Aircamper. Note classic air horn mounted outside the back cockpit.

Fig. 6-5. Small, lightweight pump used either with the hands or with the foot will inflate a small vinyl boat. Next stop: fishing!

fishing or just floating around in a lake or stream. Many of the better camping areas have water either adjoining or nearby and a small boat adds that much more to the enjoyment.

Vinyl boats with either three or four separate air chambers weigh only a fraction of the older neoprene nylon units (Fig. 6-5). The vinyl boats come in sizes from a one-man "junior" to a four-man model with four oarlocks. Thickness of the vinyl increases with the size of the boat from 14 gauge to 22 gauge. The units all have self-locking safety valves and all but the smallest have oarlocks and a rope fitted around the boat. The two-piece oars are lightweight plastic. It is reported they are unbreakable and will float.

The fishermen we've talked with report that a three-man boat is large enough for two anglers, but there is little room for the cooler that keeps the soda pop and beer at the right temperature. Some are planning to take a second "junior" and tow it to provide space for the ice chest.

Plastic foot pumps will either inflate or deflate your boat or air mattress. These are so lightweight and inexpensive that some air campers carry a spare. Manufacturers have come a long way from the old-fashioned bicycle pump that would slide all over the place when in use.

Some inflatable equipment works on compressed gasses, including the Mae West-style life jackets. Be sure that any inflatable equipment you carry in the cockpit does *not* have the carbon dioxide pressure containers installed. There is really nothing worse than having a four-man life raft slowly open and swell to full size in your cockpit. This miscue could cause a serious accident.

HOBBIES CAN ADD TO ENJOYMENT

You'll find almost as many hobbies as people. If yours happens to be archery, take your favorite bow, arrows, and a target or two. If it's golf and you still take the time to air camp, there's nothing that says you can't bring a putter and a wedge and a few brightly colored golf balls and keep your game in shape in your grassy parking area.

If you play solitaire, it goes without saying that you'll have a deck of cards along. If you crochet or work at other handicrafts, you'll have ample opportunity to keep your fingers busy, both in flight and at campsite loafing time.

We know of pilots who like to take a shovel and a pan and look for gold in the nearby creeks. Other hardy campers head for the high country when snow is on the ground and take their skis along, but that might be carrying things a bit far.

One take-along that doesn't require much space and is useful later on is a day-by-day diary. Jot down flight times for your logbook; add in fuel costs to keep track of trip cost. Add names and addresses of people you meet. List good places to stop and eat. If your camera is not fully automatic, list specific exposure data that you may want to compare with the finished photo. And don't forget a good book!

OXYGEN FOR THE HIGHER PLAYGROUNDS

If your destination is high in the mountains, you might consider some portable oxygen. We've found it a great fatigue-reducer in flights in the 8,000 to 10,000-foot levels. And if you land at a high-altitude airport after living at sea level, you can easily come up with unpleasant altitude sickness. That's where the oxygen really helps.

We landed at Steamboat Springs, Colorado, for a two-day visit. Elevation there is 6879 feet MSL and by the time you've done much unloading, walking, and unpacking, you can be much in need of a second wind. We were, and the lack of altitude acclimatization didn't do our visit a bit of good.

The Forest Service has the following information on altitude sickness. While it was prepared primarily for backpackers, the same basics apply to the air camper who visits a high altitude recreational area:

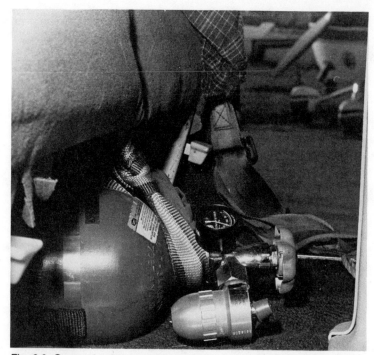

Fig. 6-6. Oxygen bottle secured beneath the front seat of the authors' Cardinal. This bottle is easily removable for refilling or to put in your tent at a high-altitude field.

"A person should spend several days getting acclimated to high altitudes before hiking. The lack of oxygen at high elevations gives some travelers altitude sickness, known as pulmonary edema, which can kill if not handled properly. The best prevention is slow ascent with gradual adjustment to altitude. Ascend no more than 2000 feet per day at elevations of 5 to 10,000 feet, then no more than 1,000 feet per day at 10 to 15,000-foot elevations. Above 15,000 feet the adjustment process is very individualized."

"Symptoms of altitude sickness are cough, lack of appetite, nausea or vomiting, staggering gait, and severe headaches. A person with symptoms of altitude sickness should breathe deeply, rest, and eat quick-energy foods such as dried fruit or candy. Take aspirin to help the headaches; antacid pills may help other symptoms. If symptoms persist, seek lower elevations immediately. Continued exposure can make the victim too weak to travel and lead to death."

We've carried portable oxygen in our Cessna (Fig. 6-6) ever since we called in at Dawson Creek enroute to Alaska a couple of years back and reported east of town when we were west. On the ground, we both had problems with simple fuel consumption mathematics. We were the second day into a long trip, short of sleep, and had spent our last two hops at 9500 feet. We headed for the motel and stopped for the rest of the day even though it was only 2:00 in the afternoon.

Since then, we've done some personal research on oxygen use in the middle altitudes and have installed a 22 1/2 cubic foot portable oxygen bottle in the Cessna. We chose a pair of Ted Nelson's economical flow meters with easy-to-read precise metering system. The Nelson system can cut oxygen use as much as 50 percent over the non-metered systems and gives the two of us an ample supply for the fuel range of our Cardinal.

On another visit to Steamboat Springs or any of the high-altitude fields in the western mountains, we'd make the oxygen available at our campsite to pep up the system when high altitude begins to take its toll. We recommend the use of oxygen in the middle altitude levels in flight, particularly before making a demanding instrument letdown. Just one word of caution: Oxygen and hydrocarbons such as lipstick make a highly combustible combination. And *don't smoke* around your oxygen mask.

When Nelson's flow meter is mounted within 20 degrees of vertical, accuracy is reported within + − 10 percent. Nelson has based his unit on tests of regular FAA-required indicators that will change from red (no-go) to green (go) with less than 1/4 liter per minute total flow. The calibrated system works against the ambient pressure to provide an accurate reading of actual usage.

The Nelson meters cost from $45.00 to $55.25 with hose and plug-in connectors. Ted Nelson is located at P.O. Box 20637, Reno, Nevada 89510.

Nelson's flow meters are designed to be accurate at the scale of the indicated altitude. Flow should be monitored during climb. Once you reach your cruising altitude, recheck the flow meter to put the floating ball exactly at your indicated altitude and then you can forget about it. At 10,000 feet, drawing one liter per minute, Nelson estimates an increased oxygen duration of 115 percent. At 15,000 feet and 1.5 liters per minute, the saving would be 40 percent. Many oxygen systems flow at 2–2.5 liters per minute regardless of altitude.

Ted Nelson is one of those prolific senior citizens of aviation. Back in the late '40s and '50s, he developed the Dragonfly and the Hummingbird motorgliders. He also developed the 50-hp H-63 engine for these two pioneering craft and still owns a Hummingbird with some 2000 hours of flight time. Nelson developed the "mizermeter," a simple and accurate pellet-type readout floating inside a transparent Lexan container. The tapered tube allows the ball to "float" higher as the flow volume of the oxygen increases. Oldtimers will remember a similar system in early sailplanes developed by Johnnie Robinson as a variometer.

However, flying with oxygen is an added chore. You've either gotta take the bottle out and get it filled, or have the FBO bring his portable cart to the flight line. That's after you find an FBO who has oxygen available with the correct fittings for your system, and a mechanic available to do the hookup. Working with oxygen bottles takes training and FBOs are reluctant to have their line boys do the filling. Pure oxygen is explosive in the presence of any grease. If you are of the persuasion to wear lipstick, wipe it off before putting on your mask.

Our procedure in refilling is for one of us to untie the bottle, put it under an arm, and take it to the line shack or hangar. Price for a 22-cubic-foot fill ranges all the way from "Well, you paid tiedown last night, so this one is on the house," to $10, $15, and $20. We've paid as high as $30 and when this fee was questioned, the comment was, "We have to pull a mechanic to do the job. It isn't how much oxygen; we'll give you a full fill in a bigger bottle for the same price."

Oxygen servicing is a hot and cold operation. One T-210 owner we contacted phoned ahead to his large FBO advising he would be in for an oxygen fill and he was assured that there was an ample supply. Later, when he picked up his ship, he found only 1400 pounds in a 2000-pound system. The shop's comment was, "Bring it back at the end of your trip and we'll top it off!"

There is little profit and considerable time expended in dispensing oxygen. You don't just taxi up to the local do-it-yourself pump and fill up your oxygen bottles, as is frequently done with aircraft fuel. Walter Cable, owner of Foothill Aircraft in Upland, California, has been dispensing oxygen for over a quarter of a century. (Cable, incidentally, holds the world class C.1-c record for nonpressurized single-engine aircraft when he took a Cessna turbo 210 to 42,344 feet over Southern California in 1967.)

Cable's shop carries oxygen with refills averaging "about $9 each." All his refilling is done by licensed A&Ps who are familiar with the hazards of handling oxygen. All are required to wash their hands and ensure that all of their tools are grease-free. In fact,

Walter's oxygen cart, which carries a bank of three large oxygen bottles out to the airplane, has special tools just for that work.

Once the customer's bottle or system is hooked up, pressure from the lowest of the three source bottles is bled into the system. For example, if you come into the shop with a 20-cubic-foot bottle like ours under your arm with 400 to 500 pounds still showing on the gauge, the A&P hooks it up, opens your valve, and fills from his lowest pressure bottle. When that pressure is stabilized, the low bottle is valved shut and the next higher-pressure bottle is opened. This continues until the top of the highest-pressure bottle is tapped. Cable's shop owns a bank of nine bottles, so there is no demurrage.

Walter Cable estimates that it takes an average of 15 minutes to fill a system because the high-pressure gas generates a great deal of heat during transfer.

Depending on their workload, some shops will use their lower-pressure oxygen bottles for welding purposes, but the gas is transferred to a yellow industrial bottle before such use and the green "breathing oxygen" bottle goes back for refilling. Acetylene, also used in welding, comes in a black bottle with fittings incompatible for oxygen containers.

When we began our research on oxygen, we asked several FAA inspectors if we would be violating any of the FARs if we purchased medical oxygen for use below 12,500 feet. We thought it might be more economical to use. (That was before we learned you need a prescription for oxygen from the local druggist.) At that time, everyone with whom we spoke (including pilots, FBOs, etc.) believed there was a difference between medical and aviation oxygen which centered around moisture content. The concensus of opinions from the FAA was that we'd be legal with medical type below 12,500 feet—but why not go whole hog with a system that could be used legally above 12,500? That made sense to us, so we did choose approved aviation equipment.

As we were finishing the material for this report, we interviewed Dr. U.A. Garred Sexton, Chief FAA Medical Examiner for the Western Region, who surprised us by saying that *all* oxygen comes out of the same container originally. If it is put in a green container, then it is okay for breathing; if it is put in a yellow container, then it's only to be used for industrial purposes such as welding. The yellow *containers* do not have the rigid standards for cleanliness that the green *containers* do.

A check with Linde, one of the largest oxygen suppliers, indicated that they package breathing oxygen in 249-cubic foot bottles filled to 2200 psi. Linde reiterated that there is no difference between aviation and medical oxygen. All containers carry the date of either their issue or their last hydrostatic testing. If the container is overdue for inspection, it will not be filled.

During our discussion with Dr. Sexton, he stated he is a firm believer in oxygen use below the required 12,500-foot limit: "When I feel a headache coming on, then I put on a mask—and that's usually at 10,000 feet. When it came to certifying pressurized airliners, the base pressure altitude of 8000 feet was chosen because the results of a study showed that at that altitude there is a decrement in the perception of light."

Dr. Sexton recommended purchase of a good mask with a microphone installed: "It's a one-time investment, so you may as well fly with the best equipment." He pointed out that regular flow control is set up for the hypothetical "average" person: "A big pilot will possibly not receive enough oxygen, while a tiny person may receive too much," he explained. "Ted Nelson's system with the ball in the tapered tube just cuts the continuous flow rate a little finer."

Because there is not a commonality in all filler connectors, Dr. Sexton advises that he carries an assortment. He stated that on several occasions the FBO did not have the correct connector for his personal oxygen system. (To date we have not had this problem with our Scott bottle.)

In March 1984, the FAA approved use of the nasal cannula (FAR 23.1447). These simple EZ/OX masks were developed by two Southern California doctors, Sidney G. White and Bernard M. Diamond. The cannula has the obvious advantage of comfort and ease of talking either into a hand mike or to passengers. Dr. White, who flew *Sundance*, the world's fastest biplane racer in 1973-74, has a military medical background dating back to WWII. He advised that the present approved cannula system makes oxygen last "almost as long as regular masks."

The FAA requires that at least one oxygen dispensing unit covering both the nose and mouth of the user be installed and available for flight above 12,500 feet "and to provide help to pilots/passengers who may have a head cold or nasal obstruction from other causes."

The White/Diamond cannulas are adapted from existing hospital equipment, weigh less than one ounce, and sell for only $6.95 each delivered. (White Diamond Corp., P.O. Box 8698,

Calabasas, CA 91302.) Dr. White stated that the new EZ/OX cannulas work well with Nelson's flow meter.

To give yourself a little more "breathing room" in the 8000 to 10,000 foot neighborhood, we'd suggest you at least rent or borrow a portable unit and give it a go. Try it—you may like it! We did.

MOTORBIKES AND BICYCLES

One of the most popular pieces of take-along equipment is some sort of ground transportation after landing. We'll discuss fold-up bicycles, minibikes, and two-piece motorcycles in Chapter 9. Your extra set of wheels can give a whole new dimension to air camping.

Chapter 7

Putting It
All Together

So it's time to drive to the airport with all your collected camping gear, load your bird, and blast off into the calm blue for an adventure in rustic living? Not yet.

WEIGHT AND BALANCE

You will want to weigh the gear that goes aboard and keep it within weight and balance. Check that old pilot's information manual on the ship you're going to fly, remembering that airplanes—like people—tend to put on weight as they get older. A radio here, a set of wheel fairings, extra instruments, seat covers, a fire extinguisher—all should be added to the basic weight of the aircraft. This is required to be done by the maintenance man who installs permanent equipment, so look up what the *present* empty weight is and go from there.

Each aircraft operations manual has its own chapter on weight and balance. For example, Piper's Dakota manual says in part: "Misloading carries consequences for any aircraft. An overloaded airplane will not take off, climb, or cruise as well as a properly loaded one. The heavier the airplane is loaded, the less climb performance it will have.

"Center of gravity is a determining factor in flight characteristics. If the CG is too far forward in any airplane, it may be difficult to rotate for takeoff or landing. If the CG is too far aft, the airplane may rotate prematurely on takeoff and tend to pitch up during climb. Longitudinal stability will be reduced. This can lead to inadvertent stalls and even spins, and spin recovery becomes more difficult as the center of gravity moves aft of the approved limit."

You will find graphs and examples of weight and balance calculations in most manuals. On the Piper Dakota, for example, the moment of the weight to be calculated is the number of inches aft of the datum point times 100. The datum point is 78.4 inches ahead of the wing leading edge at the intersection of the straight and tapered wing sections. Only the spinner and prop are forward of the datum line on this Piper (Fig. 7-1). Divide the total moment by the total weight to determine the CG location. Then add the weight of all items put into the airplane and divide the total moment to find the CG location. Locate that point on the loading graph and if it falls within the CG envelope, go fly. If not, offload and reload as required.

Believe your weight and balance figures. There's a standing joke at Mexican border airports where vacation-bound aircraft waddle up to the gas pit with considerably more weight aboard than the manufacturer permitted (Fig. 7-2). Any time that the nose wheel comes up off the ground and the tail tiedown touches the ground as the pilots deplane from the front, there's something amiss in the weight and balance. Even if nobody questions your loading or weight, it's a good bet that your insurance company won't cover you if you go out and bend your bird and they can prove you were over gross and/or out of CG.

If you're flying a taildragger, where aft loading is not as

Fig. 7-1. Piper Dakota being loaded for a camping trip. All baggage must go in the rear seats or the rear baggage compartment. Weight and balance should be calculated carefully so as not to exceed aft CG. (Courtesy Piper Aircraft Co.)

Fig. 7-2. Two-place Ercoupe at the old dirt airport at Bay of Los Angeles, Baja California, Mexico. It is not uncommon for pilots to fly into Mexico with more weight aboard than the specifications allow.

noticeable, be alert on your first full-gross takeoff for any problem in getting the tailwheel off the runway. If full throttle and full forward wheel won't raise the tail at about 20 mph, you've got a problem.

While you're working with the information manual, make sure that you have within reach a copy of the plane's checklist, all the way from walkaround to stopping the engine and parking. We carry a copy of the aircraft manual right in the Flitefile™ map case that we slipped between the front seats of our Cardinal. This prefab chart holder (from Benson Industries, Grand Ledge, Michigan) comes in six models and fits most four-place Cessnas. It helps materially to cut down on cockpit clutter.

WE LEAVE THE BACK SEAT AT HOME

If you choose to take the back seat out of a four-placer—and most serious air campers do—remember to deduct this weight from your aircraft's empty weight. This can come to 20-25 pounds that can be replaced with all sorts of goodies. In addition, removal of the back seat provides easier packing and inflight access to almost any items. And, if it ever rains so hard that you and your tent are flooded, you can always stretch out in the aft cabin, secure out of the rain and above the rivulets that always seem to run right through your tent. Of course, escaping to the aircraft cabin is admitting defeat, but sometimes you just can't get along with Mother Nature.

The four-passenger push-pull homebuilt Defiant, designed by Burt Rutan and now available in plans and prefabricated components, has a novel feature that should appeal to campers who don't like to put up tents. The back seat of this spacious homebuilt is designed so that it folds down, providing a full six-foot flat space for sleeping inside the aircraft (Fig. 7-3). The first production version of the Defiant was built by Fred Keller in Anchorage, Alaska. He and his wife have flown this twin to Oshkosh and camped out with it. Could this configuration be the air camper of the future?

CHECK IT ALL OUT FIRST

Treat all your camping gear just like you would treat your airplane. Check it out before loading. Make certain that all the parts of the tent, including pegs and enough nylon rods for the pop tent, are in the package. Assure that the propane bottles are full and that there are spares. If you had all the kitchen utensils you needed on your last trip and nobody has pirated from the pack, then you can be safe in just throwing it aboard.

AS A LAST RESORT, READ THE INSTRUCTIONS

Assuming that this is your first attempt at air camping, take the time to fully assemble all the things you have purchased. If all else fails, *read the instructions.* Some of these directions are quite detailed, but if you follow them step-by-step, you'll usually succeed. Here's what we had to do with our Stansport Super Hex Tent with fly:

Fig. 7-3. Homebuilder Fred Keller of Anchorage, Alaska, shows the amount of lie-down space available in the twin-engine Defiant he built from plans. The back seat is designed to fold down much like automotive station wagons.

"Erecting the Tent: Spread the tent floor on the ground and pull out the six corners. There are 24 fiberglass tent poles consisting of 21 with ferrules and 3 without. Separate the poles into 3 sets of 8 sections. Each set will have 7 poles with ferrules and one plain. Assemble the pole set and insert into one of the pockets (sleeve) starting at one corner making sure that the set extends from one corner through to the corner diametrically opposite. Place the emerging pole set into the corner pocket made with the 2″ webbing, allowing the balance of the pole set to protrude.

"Do this to the next two consecutive corners. When ready for erection there should be 3 consecutive corners with the pole tips inserted in the web pockets with the opposite corners having the pole sections protruding. Now grasp the protruding sections of poles starting with the last pocket assembled and slide the remaining poles into the pocket lifting the tent as you proceed (forming a hoop) until the last section can be placed into the web pocket.

"Do this with the next adjacent pole set and then to the final set. The tent is now up and at this point should be staked down at each corner using the metal stakes provided.

"Installing the Rain Fly: Locate the zipper on the rain fly and place the fly over the erected tent with the zipper over the tent door. Hook the 'S' hooks on the fly corner elastic cords to the small webbing loops extending up from the 2″ webbing loops at each corner of the tent."

"Waterproofing: Tents are made from water-repellent fabrics. However, the sewing process necessary in all tent fabrication can cause water leakage where the sewing needle perforates the fabric in the seams. For best results we strongly recommend that the new tent be erected before it is used and all seams treated with either a seam sealer or dry silicon spray."

TRIAL RUN IN YOUR BACKYARD

If you have purchased any new equipment—tent, cots, sleeping bags, stoves, or whatever—open the equipment up in the daylight and assemble it on the lawn (Figs. 7-4, 7-5). It's so much easier this way than groping in the dark with a new piece of equipment at your campsite with the wind and the rain in your hair. What a way to confound your neighbors!

In setting everything up in the backyard, go so far as to open up your sleeping bags and their pads, set up the cots, and see if everything fits inside your tent.

Fig. 7-4. Here's a backyard trial run of camping gear destined for an Alaskan trip with Freebird Tours. The tall tent in the background is a portable shower and toilet enclosure. Several types of tents were tested.

Check out the water containers to assure they haven't dried out and cracked since your last trip. Let them set overnight and then fill them with fresh water before loading.

If you're using freeze-dried or dehydrated food for the first time, why not have a cookout in the backyard with the stove you'll be taking, the water bag you'll be using, and the cooking and eating utensils from your camping gear?

Fig. 7-5. Two-burner Coleman stove is set up for testing prior to going out on a camping trip. Large coffeepot was used during group trips to Alaska by Yvonne Smith.

Shoot a couple of pictures of your backyard campout, not only as a record but to include in your photo album or color slide package. A prudent photographer will have this test roll processed and will view it carefully to make sure that both camera and film speed settings and accurate.

While it may not be a necessity, why not think about a set of wheel chocks? You can usually scrounge for rocks or branches to do the job, but it is so easy to carry your own. There are several commercial sets available from plastic or wood. We use 1 1/2" 90-degree aluminum extrusions about six inches long with each pair tied together with about 18" of light rope. Slightly larger extrusions might be better because it is possible to forget to remove them and then taxi over them with a brisk application of power. Portable tiedowns kits (Fig. 7-6) are also available.

SMALL, SOFT PACKAGES WORK BEST

The best way—perhaps the *only* way—to get the most equipment into the least space is to pack in small, soft packages rather than large, rectangular receptacles. The soft-pack material will slide easily into corners of the airplane but the bulky containers invariably create wasted space between.

"Suitcases are ridiculous," expounded our camping friend Wallace Bertram. "Take a good backpacker's frameless soft pack and you can carry 30 pounds for a couple of miles without any strain, even if you're not in the best of shape. Then you have your hands free for other chores. I used this backpack for all my travels except when flying commercial airliner; it certainly makes an easy carry from the airplane to the general aviation terminal, which can be a great distance. These frameless packs can be stored at home in a very small space, which is another advantage."

The Bertrams also recommend soft luggage rather than sharp-pointed suitcases because they hold more and don't gouge the baggage compartment of the airplane.

You may find that the glossy package that the equipment you bought came in can be eliminated and some sort of soft pack used instead. Plastic garbage bags from the corner grocery make excellent containers for many items—and you'll have the plastic bags for rain protection if worse comes to worst.

After much trial and error, we've elected to use several small cardboard boxes to pack our camping items in. They are light in weight and the smaller sizes pack easier and are easier to move within the aircraft. In loading the aircraft, we place our tent, sleeping bags, cots, and other lightweight bulky items aft. Then we place the boxes of foodstuffs and camping gear in front of these. Our personal luggage goes in next, either on top or at the side, then the camera gear—near the front for easy access during flight.

In front of the baggage compartment door we place any aircraft gear we might need for tiedown—chocks, ropes, extrusions, axe, etc. Our survival pack is loaded within reach of the pilot if quick exit becomes necessary. In front of everything, just in back

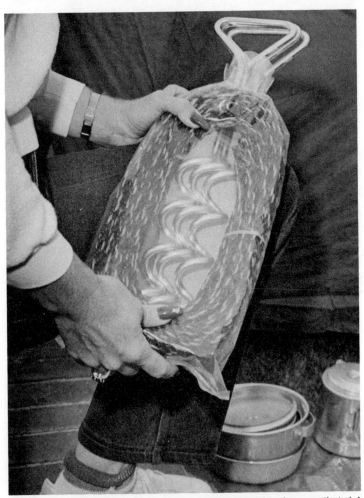

Fig. 7-6. Commercially available tiedown kits have steel corkscrews that sink into the ground. These are satisfactory except in sandy soil.

Fig. 7-7. Air camping usually goes with good weather. A Beechcraft Sierra comes in on final approach on a clear day at Gansner Field, Quincy, California.

of the front seats, is the box of charts, a supply of snacks, a container of water, and Julia's shoulderbag. This shoulderbag contains a small flashlight, sewing kit, nail file, screwdriver, "church key," insect repellent, aspirin, and various other small items that "might be needed" along the way. And yes, we do figure this into the weight and balance!

TIEDOWNS MAY BE NECESSARY INSIDE, TOO

Consider the actions of moderate or extreme turbulence on a load in the back of your aircraft. We delivered three cases of Dr. Pepper to George Escudero, manager of Hotel Las Arenas east of La Paz in Baja California. The trip down the Baja peninsula had been lumpy and some of our cargo bounced around. The cardboard containers with the canned soda were squashed flat because some cargo had shifted in flight (Fig. 7-7).

Many aircraft come from the factory with a cargo net as part of the initial equipment. Usually these are lost, strayed, frayed, or stolen over the years, but there's no problem in using netting purchased from a sporting goods, variety, or surplus store; it usually comes complete with tiedown tabs.

In any event, there is a certain sense of security with a cargo load that is tied down. In case of a sudden and unplanned stop or severe turbulence, you don't want to be wearing your camping gear. This applies particularly to bicycles, minibikes, and the small motorcycles that are becoming increasingly popular (see Chapter 9).

Chapter 8

At the Campsite

When it comes time to assemble your tent on the best available piece of high ground, protected from wind and rain as much as possible by trees, your aircraft or whatever, begin by spreading a tarp under where your tent is to go. This will keep some of the dampness out of the tent and help protect, up to a point, when/if it rains.

If you plan to stay more than a night, either by your choice or Mother Nature's, look at your tent site with the idea of being able to spread a second tarp to a wing or nearby tree to make some sort of a protected area outside the tent for this extended stay. This open space will keep friendships alive and tempers down in cases where the rain goes on forever (Fig. 8-1).

When you pick the spot to erect your tent, consider where you will have your campfire (Fig. 8-2). Tents set downwind of the fire can be showered with hot sparks that burn tiny holes in the lightweight fabric, creating an instant sieve for rain. But when you put your tent upwind of the fire, be sure to stake it down or fill it with enough weighty baggage so that it won't be blown into the fire. While good tents are treated with flame-retardant solutions, the use of an open flame with or near the tent is not recommended.

Next, set up your table, if any, or the piece of plywood that does double duty over the floor of your back area. If you're carrying a bicycle or motorcycle, put it together and get it out of the way.

Fig. 8-1. Campsite in a meadow near Lake O' Winds in Canada. Small tent is sheltered by the aircraft. Trees will also break the wind. (Courtesy Don Dwiggins)

ABOUT CAMPFIRES

Then comes the problem of picking a place for your stove or your campfire (Fig. 8-3). Whether or not to build an open fire depends on several factors. If you're in a camping area where there are prepared fireplaces, you're home free, but if the area is unimproved, there are a number of things to consider. The Forest Service has a series of handy hints on fire building in their areas that apply just as well to any open piece of ground:

1. Rely on a stove and use a campfire only when necessary.
2. Use a campfire infrequently and only when there is abundant deadwood available on the ground.

Fig. 8-2. Location of your tent will depend on what protection is available, drainage, and where you plan to build your fire.

Fig. 8-3. Four-place Beechcraft Sundowner parked beside a fireplace. Care should be taken with open fires in windy area.

3. Check with the public land management agency for local regulations. Each area may be different and regulations may change according to fire conditions.

4. Fires should be built away from tents, trees, branches, underground root systems, dry grass, and leaves. Don't build a fire near large rocks to avoid staining them with smoke.

5. If the ground is covered with needles and decomposed matter, be sure and dig through it to mineral soil.

6. Be sure the fire pit is large enough to prevent the possibility of the fire spreading.

7. Do not build fires on windy days when sparks might be dangerous, especially when the countryside is dry.

8. Select your firewood from small-diameter, loose wood laying on the ground to insure complete, efficient burning.

9. Keep water handy. Quick application will prevent fire spreading to surrounding areas.

10. Keep your fire small. A good bed of coals surrounded by rocks will give plenty of heat for cooking.

11. Never leave a fire unattended. A breeze may come up while you're gone and spread the fire [and burn your tent and your airplane!].

12. If your match is not to be thrown in the campfire, then be sure it is out. Hold until cold. Break it so that the charred portion is felt before discarding.

13. Conserve your matches. Carry a candle as a fire starter.

14. When preparing to leave your campsite, thoroughly mix water or soil with the coals and ash from your campfire. Feel the

coals with your bare hands to be sure the fire is out. Don't just bury it—it may smoulder and break out again. Make sure no roots are burning.

KEEP YOUR CAMP CLEAN

A new EPA-approved outhouse has been developed by Lou Moore Enterprises in Redding, California. It is designed to eliminate both liquid and human waste by an evaporation cycle with no sewage put into the ground, and it requires no servicing. Thus it is an ideal system to install in remote areas. Ray L. Beeninga, Superintendent of Airports for Humboldt County in northern California, is using these new outhouses in four of his remote airports and reports that they are excellent.

Human Waste

Beeninga, a longtime pilot who rebuilds Stearman biplanes for a hobby, reports that there is increasing air camping on all of the airports he supervises, with Shelter Cove along the Pacific Coastline receiving the largest number of campers. When pilots call in to ask about camping sites at Humboldt County airports, Beeninga suggest that they pick a spot along the parking area where the grass is softest and enjoy it (Fig. 8-4).

If your fly-in campsite is far enough from civilization as not to have an outhouse or trash pickup, the Forest Service has a series of suggestions on how to handle both human and camping wastes.

The proper disposal of human waste is most important. For the benefit of those people who follow, leave no evidence that you

Fig. 8-4. Aircraft with tents parked near a taxiway. Brush along the airport may be ideal padding under your sleeping bag but this area should not be used for fires.

were there; do not contaminate the waters. Fortunately, nature has provided a system of very efficient biological "disposers" to decompose fallen leaves, branches, dead animals, and animal droppings in the top six to eight inches of soil. If every camper cooperates, there will be no back country sanitation problems. The individual "cat method," used by most experienced campers, is recommended. The cat method includes the following steps:

- [ ] Carry a light digging tool, such as a plastic garden trowel.
- [ ] Select a screen spot at least 100 feet from the nearest water.
- [ ] Dig a hole 6-8 inches deep; try to remove the sod (if any) in one piece.
- [ ] After use, fill the hole with the loose soil and then tramp in the sod. Nature will do the rest in a few days or weeks.

When hiking on the trail, burial of human waste should be well away and out of sight of the trial, with proper consideration for drainage. The cat method is unnecessary for urination; however, urinate well away from trails and water resources. Use areas that are well hidden.

When staying in one campsite for several nights or traveling with a group, consider a toilet pit to minimize impact. Burning toilet paper can cause wildfires. Do not burn on the surface. Burn toilet paper only when the cat or pit method is used and there is no fire hazard. Always use caution when toilet paper is burned. If in doubt, then bury. Be sure all paper is covered with soil, rocks, limbs, or wood so it is unnoticeable and won't scatter.

Tampons and sanitary pads do not decompose quickly. They should be bagged and packed out except when in grizzly bear country (see Chapter 11). Never bury them because animals will dig them up. Burn only in an extremely hot, controlled fire.

Disposal of Camping Wastes

Keep tin cans, bottles, aluminum foil, and other "unburnables" to a minimum because they must be packed out.

Avoid the problem of leftover food by planning meals carefully. When you do have leftovers, carry them in plastic bags or bury in a remote spot well away from the campsite.

Waste water (dishwater or excess cooking water) should be poured in a corner of the firepit to prevent attracting flies. If you cook on a stove, disperse water waste far away from any body of water. Nonsoluble food particles (macaroni or noodles) in dishwater should be treated like bulk leftovers. They should be either packed up and carried out or buried in a remote spot.

Nothing should be left behind. Food scraps such as egg and peanut shells and orange peels take a long time to decompose and are an eyesore to other campers.

Fish intestines should be buried away from the water and campsite. In bear country, it is best to throw them back into the stream or as far into the lake as possible.

Monofilament line can ensnarl and kill birds. Snaps from beverage cans can cut animals or people. Animals can cut their legs on rusty tin cans. Broken glass, fishhooks, and similar trash are a hazard. Clean up these deadly discards.

Bathing and Washing

Unlike mountain men, who weren't famous for their cleanliness, today's visitors like to bathe and wash their clothes. Be aware, however, that all soap pollutes lakes and streams. Biodegradable soap does not decompose in water; it must be disposed of away from water sources. It is difficult for soil to break down too much soap in one place. Therefore, dispose of soapy water in several places or into fire ashes.

Dishes should be washed away from water sources. Dishwashing is simple; don't use soap. If food sticks, fill the pan with cold water and let it soak several hours or overnight. Clean jars or narrow-mouthed containers by shaking pebbles and water inside them. Scrub the insides of pots with sand, gravel, pine cones, or a pine needle cluster.

BEARPROOF YOUR CAMP

Should you be camping in bear country (Fig. 8-5), the Forest Service recommends that you pitch your tent as far as possible from your cooking area and your food and garbage. Try to place its door near climbable trees. The only sure way to protect your food from bears is to be smarter than they are. Suspend your food from a limb using a counterbalance system, without tying the rope to the tree. At night or anytime you are away from the camp during the day, remove all food from your pack and place it in a plastic bag in a sleeping bag stuff sack. Tie two pots or metal cups to the outside of the stuff sack to rattle and alert you if they should be moved by a bear.

Suspend the stuff sack by a rope over a medium-size branch

Fig. 8-5. Beechcraft Bonanza lands on isolated flight strip in the Sierra Nevadas. Bears may be expected in terrain like this.

(4-5 inches thick at the trunk) about 20 feet above the ground. Pull the sack up to the branch and tie a counterbalance (a rock, log or another food sack) of equal weight to the other end of the rope as high as you can reach. With a long stick, push the counterbalance upwards until both it and the stuff sack are suspended 12-15 feet above the ground, as close to the branch tip as possible, and five feet below the branch. Retrieve the food sack by pushing the counterbalance upwards until the food sack can be reached.

A clean campsite without tempting or strange odors will best ensure a night's sleep untroubled by bear visits.

IT'S CHOW TIME

Now that the shelter and fire are taken care of, it's time to think about eating. Camping food has come a long way in the past 25 or so years, with new techniques coming directly from space exploration.

Fresh Foods

Actually, your food selection will depend on what type of camping you plan to do. If you have a knockdown motorcycle or bicycle (see Chapter 9), you can carry a basic survival pack and buy fresh food from the nearest store.

If your choice of campsite is near a stream of running water and fishing is your game, you can look forward to fresh fish as a camping fare (Fig. 8-6). Freshly caught trout, fresh clams, or other seafood are great anytime, but perhaps even better when procured on your own hook or whatever. If you are fishing from one of the lightweight vinyl boats or anything else that is tippable, we'd recommend a life jacket no matter how good a swimmer you may be. Some of those streams and lakes are so cold that you have little time to function adequately.

From Your Pantry

If your plan of action for camping is to pitch your tent near the airplane and not have to make long hikes, you'll be able to use canned goods and dry packaged goods from your own kitchen shelves (Fig. 8-7). Augment these with a tour through the supermarket to choose from a variety of inexpensive packaged foods where a nominal amount of weight and space is not a problem. Noodles, hamburger helpers, cereals, soups, and packaged rice are good items.

Another technique for doing part of your cooking without working over a hot stove was shared with us by some veteran campers. This system is good for preparing your hot breakfast at the same time you're involved with cooking dinner. Use a wide-mouth thermos bottle designed to keep hot hot and cool cool (how does it know?). Virtually any of the "instant foods" are good candidates for this thermos cooking—noodles, or potato dishes, rice, freeze-dried camp foods, or dry soup mixes. The flavor may in fact be enhanced with some of these products because of the time factor involved.

After dinner, mix your uncooked cereal (instant oatmeal, for

Fig. 8-6. No matter where you catch 'em, a string of fish like this will bring a smile to any angler and improve the bill-of-fare for dinner. Aircraft is a Stinson Station Wagon.

Fig. 8-7. Campers climb through a cattle guard fence with their supplies at the old Idaho State Airport at Henry's Lake.

example) or other food with boiling water. Cook if required. Preheat the thermos before pouring in the food. Next morning you'll have steaming hot cooked cereal. Just add the brown sugar or maple syrup, the milk or cream, and you're in business.

Lightweight and Convenient

Your friendly backpacking store will have a good selection of both freeze-dried and dehydrated foods under several trade names. Mountain House is one of several well-established brands. We have used it on occasion and found it to be completely satisfactory. These packaged foods come in the basics of meat and potatoes, rice or noodles, fish or fowl, and vegetables. We did find that the friendly neighborhood rodents had found our supply in the garage and we have found a different way of storing the supplies between camping trips. We are putting them in plastic and/or metal containers rather than the old cardboard box standby.

New Packaging Methods

Recently, precooked, vacuum-sealed packaged foods have become available with a shelf life of five years without refrigeration. They bring a full gourmet style of food to your campfire with a minimum of effort (Fig. 8-8). They may be a little more expensive, but imagine that you're a hundred miles from nowhere and the cook in the party asks, "Would you rather have beef stroganoff, shrimp creole, or chicken cacciatore tonight?" And each can have his own choice in five minutes! Doesn't sound much like roughing it, does it?

Try It Before You Fly with It

No matter what combination of foods you decide on, be sure to try anything new at home before you haul it into the back country. You might not like a particular dish or a particular brand, and it is *so* much better to find this out before your trip. Plan an evening campout in the backyard. Keep track of the amount of water you use if you're going to be in an area where you must haul it in. See if your utensils are adequate; but most of all, find out if you're happy with the food.

And when the pots and pans and eating utensils come out, you'll be glad that you brought plastic plates and Teflon cooking pots. One distaff side camper advised, "We're here to play, not to scrub!"

FREEZE-DRIED AND DEHYDRATED FOODS

As we understand it, freeze-dried and dehydrated foods are

Fig. 8-8. Group campout on a Fourth of July weekend in the tiedown area at the Independence Airport (California). Many campers prefer more open area between tents.

basically the same weight but packaging is less bulky with the dehydrated material. However, in our experience, ask the average sporting goods store manager the difference between dehydrated and freeze-dried food and you'll usually get a noncommital answer with no more substance than, "You've gotta add water to the dehydrated food." So let's go a step further into the methods of processing and preserving foodstuffs. No, there's no such thing as dehydrated water!

While the various food processing measures appear quite different in application and in end products, they all approach the problem of food preservation in one or more of the following basic ways:

☐ Removal of water. Many reactions cannot occur if water is not present. Microorganisms cannot grow and multiply without adequate moisture.
☐ Heat sterilizing. Enzymes and microorganisms are destroyed or inactivated by sufficient heat. Entry of microorganisms must be prevented by suitable packaging.
☐ Lowering temperature. Most reactions slow down as the temperature is lowered.
☐ Providing a chemical environment that will not permit certain deteriorative actions to proceed.
☐ Sterizing with ionizing radiation. Special rays are used to achieve the same results as heat sterilizing (not widly used on a commercial scale).

Each of these effectively preserves certain foods, but combinations of them do an even better job. Heat sterilizing effectively destroys microorganisms, sealing in a container prevents further contamination, and storage of the canned product under refrigeration reduces deterioration normal for any canned product. Cold storage of dried products extends their storage life.

Preservation is clearly ineffective unless steps are taken to protect the processed foods from recontamination or exposure to moisture, air, or heat. The hermetically sealed can prevents entrance of microorganisms and oxygen, thus keeping the product sterile and avoiding oxidation.

Dried foods must be protected from moisture pickup, and frozen foods safeguarded against moisture loss.

Some foods must be packed in an atmosphere free of oxygen. The air may be removed or replaced by an inert gas such as nitrogen or carbon dioxide. The package is then sealed to prevent loss of inert gas and the entrance of air into the container.

In addition to the old-fashioned tin can, which is ideal as an air and moisture barrier, plastic films and laminates are used as packing materials. The laminated bag or package may contain several layers, sealed together, of an aluminum foil, draft paper, plastic film, or cardboard.

Dehydration of foods accomplishes preservation in two major ways: It removes the water necessary for growth of microorganisms and for enzymatic activity. And by removing water, it increases the concentration of sugars and acids, creating a chemical environment unfavorable to the growth of many microorganisms.

Normally, most dehydrated vegetables must be dried to a very low moisture level for reasonable stability. But the usual sundried fruits high in sugar and acids are quite stable with moisture contents from 18 to 24 percent. However, if they are dried to a moisture range of 2 to 3 percent, they are even more stable.

The cereals are quite stable at 12 to 13 percent moisture content. And the dried legumes, beans, and peas normally have moisture contents in the range of 8 to 16 percent.

Another group of foods preserved by drying are nuts. The moisture range necessary for stability is around 3 to 6 percent. The high oil content, which runs from about 48 percent in peanuts to over 70 percent in pecans, is provided with some protection from rancidity by natural antioxidants.

Nature provided man with another preserved food—sun-dried fruits. At first he probably found these preserved products under the trees, but later he reasoned that he could help matters along by picking the fruit and nuts and placing them out in the sun to dry.

Because weather is not always just right for drying cereals, legumes, nuts, and fruit, they were often spoiled and lost. So man embarked upon artificial drying, usually called "dehydration." In this process, air is heated and blown across the product. Cereals and nuts not completely dried in the field can be brought quickly to the proper moisture content in a dryer. The sun-drying of some fruits was replaced by drying in dehydration plants.

In today's kitchens, an electric dehydrating unit is a common piece of equipment. It is estimated that $50 worth of dehydrated foods purchased at the grocery store could be processed in one of these home dehydration units from $10 worth of food—and if you grow your own fruits and vegetables, the cost would be even less.

In freeze-drying, the product is kept frozen while it dries, thus avoiding the shrinkage that occurs in the course of ordinary dehydration.

A freeze-dried strawberry is just as large as the fresh strawberry, but weighs only one-sixteenth as much. Flavor changes are greatly reduced in vacuum drying. But the volatile flavoring components, like those you smell on fresh fruit, are nearly all removed—as they are in most forms of drying.

Vacuum concentration of liquids in multiple-effect evaporators is one of the least costly ways of removing water. But vacuum drying of piece-form foods—freeze-drying, for instance—is one of the most costly methods of water removal. Its use, therefore, is restricted to high-value foods—for example, meats and seasonal foods—and to military or other logistic situations demanding such lightweight dried products.

A dehydrated product remains stable only as long as it is protected from water, air, sunlight, and contaminants. Packaging, therefore, is very important.

Metal cans, plastic bags, and laminated bags and boxes effectively limit the passage of moisture and air through the package. Elimination of oxygen initially is somewhat of a problem, however. Sometimes a vacuum pack is used. Or air may be replaced with an inert gas such as nitrogen or carbon dioxide.

LABEL YOUR SUPPLIES

Should you repackage either food or drink at home for more convenient handling in your plane, be certain to mark the containers. The following is a factual account of an air camping trip that produced a number of headaches. The late Jack Leggatt, jovial editor of *Plane & Pilot, Sport Flying*, and other publications, planned to do an article on air camping with emphasis on the then-new dehydrated and freeze-dried foods. He arranged for two aircraft to fly to Cottonwood Cove, Arizona, an isolated strip along the Colorado River between Las Vegas and Bullhead City. Jack had a full load of passengers, camping equipment, and food in a Bonanza; Don was equally weighed down in a Cessna 206.

Everyone landed, secured the aircraft, unloaded the camping gear, and opened the ice cubes for happy hour (Fig. 8-9). Then came dinner time with some excellent Mountain House dehydrated food. At the time, all thought it was the fresh desert air and the sparkling stars seldom seen around big cities that caused the wonderful feeling of relaxation.

It was not until the next morning when a number of the group were comparing morning-after complaints that it was discovered that the identical unlabeled containers of clear fluid had been interchanged inadvertently, and the dehydrated food had been "undehydrated" with vodka instead of water! No wonder the aspirin flowed. (Somehow, this part of the camping adventure didn't appear in Jack's final article.).

FOIL-SEALED VACUUM PACKAGING

One of the newer space-age methods of preserving food is that employed by Yurika Foods. The processing technique used is vacuum sealing in specially designed foil packages before cooking. Thus the sealed meal is cooked in a "retort pouch" and has a shelf life of five years without using added preservatives or refrigeration. Just drop the pouch in boiling water for five minutes and it is ready to serve. And if boiling water isn't readily available, slide the pouch under the cowling while your aircraft engine is still warm. The food can be eaten without preheating if necessity so dictates because the product was thoroughly cooked immediately after sealing. This method of food preparation is a spin off of space exploration.

We were introduced to Yurika's products by pilot/backpacker Robert Jones and his wife Mildred (P.O. Box 1682, Glendora, California 91740). They are part of a nationwide group of indepen-

Fig. 8-9. Campsite at Cotton Cove, Arizona, several years ago. Note old-style heavy tents with wooden end bars. Jack Leggatt, left, supervises as others erect tents.

Fig. 8-10. Spectacular scenery like this near Jackson Hole, Wyoming, is worth all the time, expense, and effort of an air camping trip into back country.

dent distributors for the product. Look in your local phone directory for Yurika Foods under backpacking or camping equipment or contact the company in Birmingham, MI. Bob and Mildred Jones advised they would be pleased to put you in touch with your local distributor if you drop them a line. The company has 11 different entrees packaged in single-serving portions to eliminate leftovers. While we're most interested in using this product for camping trips, it would be just as good as a quick dinner at home. And the company also provides dehydrated potatoes, pastas, cereals, whey, deserts, and snacks. We have not sampled all the products, but the ones we have eaten have been excellent and they're aboard our Cardinal in our camping supplies.

About this time, if all has gone well, the sun will be lowered behind a picturesque background and you can relax and just soak up the clear atmosphere (Fig. 8-10). If so inclined, you can also soak up a tall cool one or two. Open up the camp chairs and enjoy.

Chapter 9

Wheels after Landing

An airplane is great transportation and a wonderful way to have a good look at our countryside. However, there has always been one drawback: once you land, you're fresh out of transportation. In big cities you can pick up a rental car, go into hock for a cab, choose your motel with a courtesy car service, or even ride the bus. In the back country, you just don't have these options.

Today, many air campers take their wheels with them—either a motorbike, motorcycle, or bicycle. Putting a cut-down small motorcycle in the back of your four-place plane has been one of the greatest aids to successful air camping. It makes it a whole new ballgame!

If you have any sort of a bike, either pedal or powered, you can plan an entirely different style of air camping. Only on rare occasions are you so far away from civilization that you can't ride to a small general store for fresh meat and vegetables or that forgotten necessary item.

BICYCLES ARE A BIG HELP

Let's start out with the simplest airborne wheels. Perhaps the least pretentious showed up in, of all places, the ultralight section of the annual EAA Fly-In at Oshkosh. David Sadowski of Milwaukee, Wisconsin, was flying his Pterodactyl Ascender with his ten-speed bicycle securely tied to the kingpost (Fig. 9-1). He

Fig. 9-1. David Sadowski has this 40-pound ten-speed bike tied atop the wing during The EAA Fly-In at Oshkosh, Wisconsin.

reported that the drag of the 40-pound bike was negligible when attached to his slow-speed ultralight.

There are many types of bicycles suitable for folding into the back of your airplane. If you're a do-it-yourselfer, it is a relatively simple matter to cut your existing bike in half and add a set of fittings to hold it rigid again when reassembled.

Simple clamps are on the market that offer a separation kit for either standard men's or women's two-bar bicycles (Fig. 9-2). John F. Benson, the developer (P.O. Box 312, Glendora, California 91740) says, "All you need is a hacksaw to cut the bike in half, and an electric drill to drill four holes. The separation adapters have a built-in stop and a predrilled hole. Merely slip the adapter in place and drill through the tubing. Then push the other half of the bike into the coupling and drill again. Insert the bolt with a wing nut attached and tighten."

Benson advises that in some cases, it is necessary to loosen the handlebar and seat for a minimum package. For use with three-speed or ten-speed bikes, the developer says that the rear caliper brake lever and the gear shift lever must be removed from the handlebar and remounted under the seat so that the wires will not interfere with separation. Benson's adaptors come in 16″, 20″, 24″, and 26″ sizes with the 24″ bike the smallest he recommends for pedal power (Figs. 9-3, 9-4). And don't forget the rack on the back to carry suitcases or groceries.

Fig. 9-2. John F. Benson with a cut-in-half bicycle folded to fit in the back of his Cessna 182. He sells the fittings to reassemble the bike.

The tandem bicycles built for two can also be sectioned, but into three units. The two-seaters take up considerably less baggage space than two individual units.

Check with your local bike shop for both conventional bicycles to cut down or to ascertain if powered bikes are available in your area. Benson says that Sears sells a superbly designed 13-pound

Fig. 9-3. A small 20-inch bike is shown assembled with Benson's separation kit installed.

Fig. 9-4. Benson pedals a small bike past the nose of his Cessna at Brackett Field, La Verne, California. Two removable clamps are used to reassemble the bike from two parts after unloading.

engine that can attach to the front wheel of 20″ and larger bikes. It can be mounted in minutes and "clutched out" so that the bike can be pedaled in the normal manner.

One of the lightest fold-up bikes was designed by Harry Bickerton, formerly chief engineer for deHavilland and Rolls-Royce. His product is a three-speed machine with small diameter wheels that weighs just 24 pounds. The designer says that it unfolds from a handbag size in just one minute. Distribution is by Lightrider Cycles, Ltd., P.O. Box 718, Lakeville, Connecticut 06039.

Another of the several companies specializing in bicycle conversions is BikeAlong™ of Rt. 1, Box 303, Marsh, Wisconsin 53936. They recommend a standard-sized 12 speed 27″ unit that can be shipped by UPS. BikeAlong reports that its units are even used by apartment dwellers who have insufficient room for a completely assembled bike.

A goal of bike modifiers like John Benson is to develop a low-cost 50-pound bike, motorized, capable of carrying 450 pounds and luggage, which folds into a briefcase. "We're working on it," said Benson as he looked at the small modern machine in his hangar at Brackett Field, east of Los Angeles.

MOPEDS FOLD UP, TOO

Powered bicycles come under the moped laws in most states

and do not require special licenses. The engines will deliver 200 to 300 mpg at speeds of 20 to 25 mph. Oil (2 percent) must be added to the gas (av/gas will do). Power is delivered directly to the front wheel and gives the same performance regardless of the size of bike wheel. Total weight is about 65 pounds (Fig. 9-5).

A number of years ago on a visit to Bermuda, we found bikes of this type were extremely popular since there were no full-sized automobiles permitted on the island at that time. As I remember it, the trade name on the bikes was Vespa and they were remarkably easy to ride.

There are a few electric bikes on the market that use a standard aircraft battery for power. However, they will deliver only 11 miles per charge at about 17 mph. Because of their short range and somewhat heavier weight, these units have not become particularly popular with air campers.

MOTORCYCLES FLY ALONG

If your airplane is as large as a Cessna 182, you can pick up a Honda Trail 70 that weighs 148 pounds and will fit in the back of the aircraft without disassembly. The four-cycle engine will run on av/gas. John Benson has one of these in his Cessna Skylane and reports that the Trail 70 will pack two people without difficulty. He recommends getting a set of old-style handlebars from a wrecking yard so that breaking down the assembly is not necessary (Fig.

Fig. 9-5. Moped installation on the front handlebars of a lightweight bike. These units will deliver 200 to 300 mpg.

Fig. 9-6. John Benson wheels his small Honda Trial 70 up the special ramp he has built for his Cessna 182. Note that the ramp is fitted under the landing wheel to clear the wheel fairing.

9-6). Benson has built a foldable aluminum extrusion ramp to roll the Trail 70 in and out of his ship without becoming entangled with the wheel fairings.

There's really nothing new about air camping with a Cessna 150. Back in the early 1960s we met a retired midwest businessman (Fig. 9-7) who was a flying "snowbird." Living alone in the midwest winters, he packed his gas stove and meager camping gear into his not-new Cessna 150 and headed for the Southwest. We met him in the parking area at Furnace Creek in Death Valley. His aircraft cabin had been modified so that he had an air mattress and a sleeping bag stretching down into the fuselage, eliminating the need for a tent. He had a tiny small-wheeled motorbike to get from the airport to town. Because he was living on a fixed income, he knew which bakery in Bishop had the best day-old bread, which airport had the best rates on fuel, and which meat market ground the best economy hamburger. This early air camper would come to the warm Southwest every winter for six weeks to two months during the worst of the midwest winters. Then he would fly home to spend the summers in his city apartment. He felt that he had the best of two worlds on a minimum budget.

A TWO-PART HONDA

We first heard of John Beecher of Miles City, Montana, and his cut-down Honda 90 (Fig. 9-8) from a report in the Cessna Cardinal Association newsletter. He provided us with photos and a full package of how-to-do-it information because "I hope it will dispel the myth that flying is just for those who can afford expensive motel rooms and rental cars." He continued: "Last summer was our first with our converted Honda. We took mostly day trips getting used to it in the plane and were careful and cautious. We took one overnight camping trip to Hardin, Montana, and rode the 40 miles round trip to the Custer Memorial on the Honda. We would not have wanted to do it on a bicycle and no other transportation was available.

John Beecher describes how he altered his Honda thusly: "We finally cut our Honda motocycle in half that we bought new last summer. It wasn't easy to take a brand-new cycle to a welding shop and tell the guy to cut it in half, but we have no regrets.

"We had planned this for five years, ever since I saw someone take two halves of a Honda 90 out of a Cessna 170 at a fly-in in May of 1978. First we had to get our Cessna 150 paid for and then trade it in on a plane large enough to carry a motorcycle. After making payments on our Cardinal for 1 1/2 years, we could afford to purchase a Honda last year. After trying out the Honda for a year to make sure we wanted to keep it and cut it in half, we took it

Fig. 9-7. "Snowbird" from the midwest with his Cessna 150 is shown tied down on the Furnace Creek Airport, -221 feet AGL. He used this tiny motorbike to travel from the airport into town.

108

Fig. 9-8. John Beecher of Miles City, Montana with the front half of his Honda 90 beside his 150-hp 1968 Cessna Cardinal. (Courtesy John Beecher.)

Fig. 9-9. Honda 110 (formerly 90) with the plastic cover and chrome engine guard removed prior to cutting the tube that connects front and rear. (Courtesy John Beecher)

to the hospital and had it operated on. Our only regret is that we didn't do it *last* summer."

The Cardinal owner chose this particular motorcycle because it has to be cut in only one place. He used four 9/16" one-inch long bolts to hold the front and rear of the bike together for riding. Two quick-disconnects were used on the wiring where it runs along the neck of the motorcycle. All the wires (about 15) can be connected or disconnected in not over two seconds, according to Beecher (Figs. 9-9 through 9-11).

Beecher removed the rear seat from his Cardinal to carry the motorcycle. A car ramp is placed under the rear half of the bike in the airplane and is used for loading and unloading the Honda. These car ramps are available at discount stores for about $15 per pair when on sale, according to Beecher. He also uses a pair of 2" × 7' boards to help roll the rest of the cycle in and out of the cabin.

The luggage rack on the motorcycle is standard and strong enough for lifting or securing the Honda. An optional passenger seat costs about $25 and can be attached easily. The mirrors, throt-

Fig. 9-10. Rear half of the Honda including engine as it was mounted in the back of the Cessna Cardinal. Rear seat had been removed. Car ramp is placed under the motor. (Courtesy John Beecher)

Fig. 9-11. Both halves of the Honda resting in the back of the Cardinal. A tarp is on the floor to protect the cabin. (Courtesy John Beecher)

tle cable, and handlebars are all set up for quick release as standard equipment. There is no clutch cable because the clutch is automatic. When mounted in the cabin, the handlebars are turned parallel to the front tire. The Honda has dual kickstands that allow the rear half to remain self-supporting while the front half is removed and loaded into the plane first.

The Honda 110 Trailbike (formerly Honda 90 in the older models) has four speeds in both high and low range. Beecher says, "Yes, it really does have a two-speed transmission with a total of eight gear ranges and will climb straight up the side of a mountain with two people if you can stay on it. It will cruise at 45 mph with two people aboard."

There are holes for tiedown rings already in the floor of the Cardinal. The owner reports that "Cessna sells tiedown rings for $16 each, but we had 1/4″ fine-thread eyebolts made by a welder in a machine shop for $1.33 each. A commercial welder did the complete cutting job, including wiring and touch-up paint on the Honda for $48. Eyebolts, including two extras, cost $8. Four quick-release motorcycle tiedowns straps were $20. Four black rubber bungees, $4. Total cost of modification and tiedown gear was $80.

The step-by-step loading procedure is described by the Cardinal owner as follows:

"To secure the motorcycle, four motorcycle tiedown straps are hooked to the four eyebolts in the flow of the plane and then all are attached to the luggage rack under the rear seat of the Honda. Now the rear wheel cannot move but the motor can still shift left-to-right. This lateral movement was eliminated by attaching two black rubber bungees with hooks to two holes in the square flange and then to the eyebolts at each door post.

When the front half of the cycle is placed into the Cardinal, the tire ends up located next to a tiedown ring which is located high on the side of the fuselage next to the hatshelf. A short black rubber bungee is wrapped around the tire and fastened to this tiedown ring. To secure the remainder of the front end to the side of the passenger compartment, a very long black rubber bungee is hooked to this same tiedown ring, laid across the fork and handlebars, and then hooked to the eyebolt on the floor next to the door post."

In field operation, Beecher removed the main gear wheel pants for greater ease in loading and unloading. With the rear seat and wheel pants removed, Beecher says, "Our Cardinal with full fuel carries my wife and me (300 pounds), motorcycle and related gear (240 pounds), and 100 pounds of luggage and camping gear. Of course, we will not carry full fuel with a load like this at high density altitude. The Honda weighs 210 pounds with a gallon of gas in it.

"There is a quick drain for carburetor and fuel lines to prevent broken lines and seals from expansion at altitude," said the Cardinal owner. "By using the fuel shutoff valve and the quick drain, all fuel is contained within the Honda gas tank. This is especially important on an older model, which may have worn-out fuel lines or gaskets that could burst at high altitudes. I do not recommend flying the Honda with a full tank of fuel in order to prevent the venting of fumes into the cabin. There is no need for it because one gallon of gas is two-thirds of a tank and will last 90 miles.

"There is a real honest-to-goodness spare gas tank on this Honda for your trips into the back country, but I leave it at home to save weight when using the motorcycle in the plane," said Beecher.

"One must be careful with density altitude in the mountains with two people and the Honda in our plane, which is a 150-hp 1968 Cardinal. A 180-hp would be better, but we cannot afford one and hope that one day we'll be able to use auto fuel legally in ours, so we plan to keep it. Besides, we love the plane."

The economies of this cut-up Honda are evident. The Beechers can load and unload their motorcycle, including setup, in 20 minutes. They note that "it takes that long to rent a car, but you'll only spend a dollar for a weekend on your Honda, instead of $70 for a rental car. Can the average pilot ride a bicycle through the Rocky Mountains on a weekend outing with his spouse? I doubt it, but we can do it on our Honda."

BIKES FOR THE FILMMAKERS

Nearly a decade ago, when Bob and Marian Auburn were producing their excellent travel films for Beechcraft, they carried two sizes of motorbikes in addition to their camera gear. One was a full-sized lightweight dirt bike capable of carrying two people and their poodle (Fig. 9-12). The other small-wheeled Honda was useful for scouting camera locations.

Fig. 9-12. Bob and Marion Auburn with their poodle aboard a small motorbike on an isolated dry lake on the west coast of Baja California. This bike was carried in their accompanying Cessna 180.

113

Fig. 9-13. Don Downie prepares to test hop the tiny Honda bike on a Baja California dry lake. Bob Auburn gives preflight instruction.

We met up with the Auburns on an isolated dry lake on the West Coast of Baja California just south of Punta Abreojos (eyes open). At the time of our Baja meeting, the Auburns were using two airplanes on their filming projects. The then-new Bonanza was the target airplane and a Cessna 180 with wing-mounted, remote-triggering 16mm cameras was used as the photography platform. Each member of the filming team was qualified in either airplane and as camera operator or lead pilot.

We watched their filming and tried the midget Honda on for size (Fig. 9-13). Because we were a long way from the nearest hospital where a bent or broken leg could be set, our trials with the little bike were limited to very slow speeds. It was fun and the usefulness of this type of transportation when there just isn't anything else for miles and miles is self-evident.

For a detailed report on how three couples in three Cessna 182s and three cut-in-half Hondas air camp, see Chapter 10.

Chapter 10

As Others
Have Done It

There's great variety in the wild, wonderful world of air camping. Pilots flying solo in small homebuilts and economy antiques and classics putt-putt from airport to meadow, extremely content with the personal isolation of it all. Then couples with conventional aircraft explore the back country with more speed and perhaps more comfort. Some add the accessories of bikes, powered or unpowered. And some like to plan combined trips with other flying friends. Take the exploits of three couples at our home field, Cable Airport in Upland, California.

THREE CESSNA 182S, THREE HONDAS, AND SIX PEOPLE

We sat in the corner of Duane and Peggy Binnall's small hangar at Cable Airport and talked about flying in groups. Two other couples, Carmen and Amy D'Antonil and Cecil and Pat Stokesberry, joined the hangar-flying session. All three couples own Cessna 182s and all carry Hondas in place of the back seat. All three men are instrument rated, two of the wives have soloed, and the third is planning to take at least enough training to solo. However, the wives all keep busy with copilot duties: map reading, frequency selection, navigation, and sometimes sleep. Pat Stokesberry has recently discovered videotape cameras and preserves their group camping flights for later projection.

These avid campers—let's dub them the "Cable Campers"—

Fig. 10-1. Duane and Peggy Binnall unload their Cessna 182 in preparation for setting up camp.

love to fly; they seek grassy strips and abhor control towers. They aver that it takes a certain type of person to camp—one who has an affinity for the great out-of-doors.

"Half the fun is in the camping," said Carmen. "We look for the remotest area we can fly to. I like to camp and that's the best way to get away from things," he explained. "Sitting in a motel in front of the TV is really no different from being at home." (Figs. 10-1, 10-2)

Fig. 10-2. The tent is up, the Honda assembled, and the "Rubber Duck" being inflated by the Binnalls.

Each of the couples had camped out before learning to fly and they use their airplanes as an extension of their radius of action. "It's really a fun way to vacation," they said. "We may start out with a game plan to go to A-B-C; but if we fly over a promising grass strip along the way, our plans go out the window." Interplane communication makes a meeting of the minds easy to accomplish in flight.

"If we are at a towered field, we'll call for taxi as a flight of three and advise that we'll maintain our own separation. It's surprising how many towers will okay a formation takeoff if you ask them casually as you're taxiing out," the trio advised.

Because they are based in Southern California, it is predictable that some of the favorite destinations of the Cable Campers are in the cooler, greener Pacific Northwest. Two favorite airports in this area are Concrete and Tieton (French Farms) in the state of Washington. When the three Cessnas landed at Concrete, the part-time airport manager brought out a power mower and cut the grass in the area where the visitors wanted to camp. Concrete has a 2700-foot strip at 260 feet MSL less than a mile from town. There is running water in the tiedown area.

When the Hondas (Fig. 10-3) were assembled and the Cable group headed for town, the airport manger said, "Be sure to tell everyone in town that you are pilots and you're using the airport!"

Tieton is normally a one-way strip with an overwater approach. Elevation is 2134 feet MSL with only a 1700-foot grass and dirt strip. This strip is a little short for the Cable group's preference, but it is a one-way strip with a slope to the west and a zero approach so that the 182s handle it without much of a problem. Nor-

Fig. 10-3. Duane and Peggy Binnall head for the nearest stream with their Solar inflatable boat atop the Honda--unwieldy, perhaps, but it works.

mally, the Cable Campers limit their group flights into airports with runways at least 2200 feet long with good, clean approaches.

Other northwestern sites popular with the Cable crew are Rick's at Sandy, Oregon and Lester, one of the suburban strips maintained by the State of Washington. Lester is variously reported as being 2200 feet long, 1639 feet MSL, closed in the winter, surface rough, tall grass, trees and mountains for obstructions, and use at your own risk. Pedestrians, vehicles and animals may be on the runway. At Sandy, Oregon, there are three strips to choose from in this area 25 miles west of Mt. Hood. One has an asphalt runway; two are turf. The Cable Campers prefer Rick's where both fuel and maintenance are available.

The trio of Cessna drivers tries to fly no more than three hours a day because these are vacation trips. On a typical junket, they will depart Cable nose-to-tail (if the runway is wide enough, they take off in formation) so as not to waste time in getting together in the air. First stop on one trip was Columbia, California, a short hop, where excellent camping facilities are available. Next stop was Garberville in northern California, where camping facilities are also available. This puts the Washington-Oregon back country strips within a half-day's flight.

The Cable Campers are always on the lookout for a level, grassy spot on which to pitch their tents. They advise that on close-in airports, there isn't much room for selection. However, when conditions permit, they park the three Cessnas as close together as possible and then stretch tarps between the wings for protection from sun and wind. However, when they hit rainy weather, this trio usually has an alternate and go to it. They carry rain gear. They consider ponchos better than conventional lightweight raincoats.

Each couple carries a cut-in-half Honda 90 (all 187 pounds of it). Binnall admits that he is not a biker and will not ride the little Honda in a city. He considers the 90cc Honda to have minimum horsepower for two people. "You can't go on the freeway with it," he commented, "but it is great for going to town for groceries or putting around to look at the scenery or to find a laundromat. It also is quick transportation from the airplane to the motel. Having the Honda makes the logistics of air camping ever so much easier."

Although Binnall says that it's possible for one person to extract his two-piece Honda 90 from the back of his 182, he and his wife can do it together much more easily. They can assemble the bike in less than seven minutes without hurrying. Some owners of 182s can fit the later-model Honda 90 in the back seat area without

Fig. 10-4. Cable Campers plan a trip. Left to right are Pat and Cecil Stokesberry, Amy and Carmen D'Antonil, and Peggy and Duane Binnall. The Binnall's Cessna 182 is in the background.

disassembly, but they usually carry a ramp to load and unload the machine.

Care should be taken to tie down heavy items of camping gear so that they won't fly around the aircraft cabin in rough air. "I'm very careful with the Honda," said Binnall. "I don't want to be wearing it. I use tiedown clips bolted into the back seat brackets and nylon cord to secure the vehicle."

"You must pick your traveling companions very carefully," said Duane Binnall(Fig. 10-4). "There's a lot of togetherness. The six of us get along well. We pick comfortable spots where the fishing is good. Most of the Pacific Northwest areas we use are what you'd call 'clean camps' with moderate temperatures and no dust. We can go four or five days comfortably without a motel. But a laundromat after about three days is welcomed."

The three wives say that they can keep clean using just a soup bowl of warm water and a hand towel. All three women feel that it is very important to use some makeup every day while camping. Cecil, who wears a full beard all the time, wisecracked, "I never shave when I'm camping." Neither do the other men.

There is an unwritten law that any of the group can break away and do whatever they wish at any time. For example, after a stop in Washington, one plane went to Portland, one went to Vancouver, B.C., and the third went 80 miles north to Morton. They reunited for the trip south two days later.

The Binnalls say that the three-man inflatable solor boat call-ed "Rubber Duck" is just a little small for two people, fishing tackle, and ice chest. They plan to experiment with a very small additional pump-up raft to tow along for the ice chest and fishing tackle boxes.

When the trio of 182s go out together, each is self-sufficient, but there is some group planning on frying pans and pots to eliminate bulky/heavy duplication. The group uses plastic plates with one each knife, fork, and spoon. Small dishes stack one atop the other.

Each plane carries two folding beach chairs. "These are very important," said Binnall. Each uses a 42" × 32" × 1/4" plywood floor cover for the back of the airplane on which to set their break-down Honda. After the bike comes out, the plywood serves as a tabletop. Propane stoves are preferred, inexpensive $14.95 units. Stokesberry had a small backpacker's "grasshopper" stove that he finally broke after 10 years; he replaced it with the simple pro-pane unit. Regarding new equipment, the group said, "If it needs a trial run, don't buy it. If it breaks, don't bring it home."

Cooking with the Cable Campers can be innovative. It ranges all the way from hot dogs and chili to packaged beef stroganoff. Prepackaged oatmeal, usually with raisins, makes a good, quick breakfast. Wild blackberries, frequently found near northwest air-ports, make a great breakfast, according to the Campers. "Once we got caught in a cornfield near an airport in Washington," said Bin-nall. "The owner drove by and hollered, 'They're not ready yet.'" The group report that everywhere they have gone so far, people have been gracious, and they are amazed when the Hondas come out of the aircraft. Permission to camp has never been a problem.

In campgrounds where permanent potties are not available, Mother Nature calls for a trip into the brush with a shovel. One of the feminine trio noted, "It didn't take me long to learn to select a piece of sloping ground and face uphill." Water is carried in 2 1/2-gallon plastic fold-up containers.

When it came to a discussion of the economics of air camping, the Cable Campers noted the savings of no motel fees and no rental car fees with their Hondas (Fig. 10-5). However, if you were really to amortize what you'd spend on camping gear, you'd be able to stay in a pretty good motel. When we save $50 per night on a motel, that's just another 20-25 gallons of gas to extend our trip. Because all three Cessnas are powered with 80-octane engines, the ground is looking forward to the legal availability of auto gas.

On one recent trip, Cecil broke a bone in his hand when his

Honda took over and put him into a small tree. After the hand was set in a plaster cast, specially cut so that he could hold the control wheel, Duane Binnall took him around the field a couple of times to make sure Cecil could handle the controls properly, and then the three planes continued on their planned three-week trip. Pat helped with the camping and things went along fine until the group found a spot with good fishing. Cecil found out promptly that he couldn't reel in his catches, but Pat handled that.

On short overnighters, the Cable group congregate at one of the hangars on a Friday evening during the long summer nights. Someone decides where to go within a reasonable distance and anyone else on the field who wants to tag along is welcomed. However, on the longer trips, the three Honda-carrying Cessnas pretty much stick to themselves.

A typical Fourth of July weekend will find the three Cable Cessnas parked in the corner of the Prescott, Arizona, airport with the Hondas ready for the short drive to the annual Rodeo.

Even though the Cable Campers have cats and dogs, they line up a "house sitter" and leave their pets at home. While the group enjoys the economies of their air camping junkets with the Hondas, they freely admit that their back country trips are dictated

Fig. 10-5. Hondas like this are flown by many air campers to save money and open up new areas for exploration—and a quick trip to the country store. Duane Binnall assembles his Honda.

much more by the uncluttered terrain than any real cost saving.

Now, when it comes to the cost per pound of one freshly caught trout, that's expensive! However, the group's next planned trip is to a field near the Montana-Idaho border where they'll hike to a lake where there are reports of 63 fish, all over eight pounds, being caught in just three hours. Where exactly is it? The group just grinned.

SANTA CLAUS IN A BELLANCA

One of Wallace Bertram's most memorable camping trips goes back a number of years. He and his 1939 14-19 Bellanca were with a group of three other aircraft, all headed for Rancho Buena Vista near the tip of Baja California, Mexico, with Christmas presents for the children in a nearby village. The flying caravan hit a blinding rainstorm near El Barril some 80 miles south of Bahia de Los Angeles, and there was no alternative but to land. Bertram was the first to land and had to use his landing lights to search out a wide spot on the dirt road that served as a runway. The following aircraft landed with illumination from his lights.

The planes were loaded with toys that had been rejected by the Mattel Company's quality control department and were promptly given to the children of El Barril.

"Those kids had never seen a toy in their lives," said Bertram. "The talking dolls were an instant hit. Later we brought down some Spanish educational material and coloring books for the children there and at San Borjas, an old mission with a terrible flight strip at that time. When we started these flights, the children weren't even going to school, but that was quite a while ago. In recent years, the situation has improved and schooling is available."

LAKE MINCHUMINA AND THE GREAT OUTDOORS

On one of our trips through Alaska, we decided to camp at Lake Minchumina on the North Fork of the Kuskokwin River between McGrath and Fairbanks. Years ago, it was the site of an FAA station and is now used by the BLM air tankers. The state maintains a few camping tables and a latrine at the end of Runway 29. There is the wreckage of a C-46, which attempted a takeoff with its controls locked, in the traffic pattern.

We landed on the smooth gravel strip, pulled off, and drove our tiedowns into the ground. It was a beautiful area, completely deserted and just like the travel brochures. After putting up our

Fig. 10-6. Julia Downie uses a camping table provided by the State of Alaska to cook dinner at Lake Minchumina. The tent is on the other side of the airplane.

tent and pulling our stove and food box out of the back of the Cessna, we replenished our mosquito repellent—Cutters, of course—and relaxed (Fig. 10-6).

After a tall cool one, we rigged up a fishing line and went after the famed pike that were reported in the lake—maybe so, but we had nary a bite. We threw flat pebbles into the water, breathed in the scenery, looked out toward towering Mt. McKinley, and finally cooked a good dinner.

It began to rain, but that's par for the course when you camp in this part of the world and we were protected by the high wing of the Cessna. It really doesn't get dark in Alaska in the summer, but eventually we climbed into our pop tent, sprayed for mosquitos, and hit the sack. It was peaceful and isolated. We felt we had really gotten away from civilization.

At about 4 A.M. the serenity was shattered by the landing of a Cherokee 6 with a full load of fisherman, complete with rubber boat and even an engine. Within the next two hours, there were four more charter planeloads of fishermen. It seems that we had selected a popular fishing spot for the residents of both Fairbanks and Alaska when they want to get away from it all.

We swapped lies with each succeeding loads of pilots and finally packed up our gear to head back to Fairbanks. Minchumina is a great place to visit, perhaps even to fish, but it sure didn't turn out to be complete isolation.

OSHKOSH; BIGGEST CAMPOUT OF THEM ALL

Everything about the EAA's annual Fly-In held at Oshkosh, Wisconsin, the first week in August every year is big. There are over 14,000 aircraft on one field at one time, up to 300,000 visitors on the field for the Sunday show alone, up to 800,000 visitors dur-

Fig. 10-7. Photo from an EAA helicopter shows rows and rows of parked aircraft camping at Oshkosh. Aircraft parking is on both sides on the runway, with some 11,000 aircraft on the field at one time.

ing the week, and an estimated $36 million of revenue to the economy of this friendly Wisconsin town. There are also 5000 air campers (Fig. 10-7), according to EAA estimates. Some afficionados come early and stay late. Others may fly in for just one night or two.

The transient parking area for modern aircraft is over 55 rows deep with 20 or more aircraft per row, depending on size, high or low-wing, and compactness of parking. That's well over 1000 camped airplanes in one lot on the south side of Runway 9/27. Add the tents erected by arrivals in the regular transient parking area and the show aircraft camping area west of Runway 18/36, and you'll have easily 3000 aircraft campers at one time (Fig. 10-8).

The Oshkosh Fly-In has been going for a long time; the 32nd annual Fly-In was held in 1894. With this history to work from,

Fig. 10-8. All sizes and shapes of tents are visible in this low-altitude helicopter photo at Oshkosh.

124

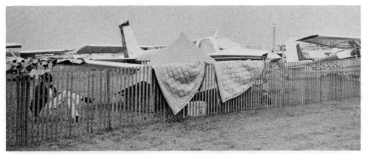

Fig. 10-9. Bedding hanging out to dry after a wet night at Oshkosh.

it's no wonder that they are set up properly. Visitors find two complete country stores with camping supplies at each of the two formal camping areas. The main cafeteria with full means is open from 5:30 A.M. to 10:00 P.M. plus smaller cafes in the Warbirds area, the Chicken Cafe, a steak house, plus cafes near the tower and in the classic aircraft parking area.

In all, there are 16 foot outlets on the airport during the week. Shuttle buses, either free or with a small donation pick up at all campsites and bring campers to the flight line. City buses run at frequent intervals.

Tiedowns are required, and if the visitor has forgotten his, they are available for the week on a $15 refundable deposit. EAA crews patrol the areas to assure that all aircraft are tied securely because the chances are that at least once during the first week of August there will be a howling storm with wind, rain, and spectacular lightning come through the area. A surprisingly few aircraft have been uprooted and damaged. However, the morning after the rainstorm is another matter (Figs. 10-9, 10-10). Most campout planes have bleeding and mattresses draped over the wings, tail, and prop for drying. Those who have spent the night out in these

Fig. 10-10. Cardinal in the foreground has bedding over both wings to dry. Spartan Executive, one of the many classic aircraft at Oshkosh, taxis by in the background.

125

Fig. 10-11. A portion of the thousands of air campers that congregate at the EAA Fly-In at Oshkosh every year.

weather conditions later get together and swap storm stories by the hour. Some of these accounts vie with the stores about flying into Oshkosh on the first two days of the event, when aircraft are handled beautifully by volunteer FAA air traffic controllers: "Don't call us. Just follow the plane ahead of you." Aircraft are landed sometimes four at a time on a single wide runway—one long, one short, one right, one left—with almost no miscues. It is one of the best shows at Oshkosh just to watch the arrivals—and from what better spot than on a camp chair under the wing of your plane with your tent and sleeping bags ready for the evening?

In 1984, the campout charge was $8 per night per plane. Showers, toilets, water, and telephones are provided in each of the camping areas. One section of the field is marked off for homebuilts who have camping equipment. Antiques (built before 1946) and Classics (those licensed aircraft build between 1946 and 1955) are parked in another area. Two huge sections are reserved for campout "Spamcans," as some EAAers call factory built aircraft.

A visit to Oshkosh is the best single way to get your feet wet (Fig. 10-11); sometimes quite literally you'll get your feet wet in air camping. If and when you visit the Oshkosh Fly-In, you'll have the opportunity to see just about every type of tent, sleeping bag, tarp, or other equipment that has ever been developed or conjured up. And, when you camp at Oshkosh, you're right in the middle of where all the action is.

Chapter 11

Unscheduled Landings

There's one basic difference between air camping and survival after an unscheduled landing: The latter wasn't your own idea. You had other things planned: appointments, a job to return to, friends and relatives expecting you, and all that. However, for one of a number of reasons, you didn't make it.

Unscheduled landings are usually caused by weather, low fuel, or maintenance problems. Utilizing Murphy's Law, they occur at the most inopportune time and at the most inopportune place—all of a sudden, you've gotta land! However, most forced landings do give the pilot *some* warning. The oil temp goes up and the pressure down; the fuel gauges begin bouncing on that big "E" or the weather in front of you goes from bad to worse. It gets so dark or hazy that you can't see enough to continue VFR. Whatever the cause, you will probably have some warning. Engines that disintegrate, props that fly off, and pieces of structure that suddenly come unglued fortunately are a rarity.

SUGGESTED TECHNIQUES

The mechanics' and gamblers' odds on forced landing techniques are varied and no two suggestions will work every time. However, there are a few basic rules. Make your "Mayday" call as early as possible and crank in a 7700 code on your transponder if there is one aboard. If your ELT has a remote switch or is

Fig. 11-1. With a modern airplane, it is a simple matter to be a long way from civilization in just a few minutes. This Piper Arrow is shown near Mt. Whitney, 14,495 feet MSL in the High Sierras. A forced landing in country like this could require a good survival kit.

mounted where you or a passenger can reach it, turn it on in the air (Fig. 11-1).

Personally, we monitor the Flight Watch weather frequency of 122.0 on our No. 2 radio and almost always will have another aircraft within range. As a personal preference, we recommend a call there and worry about the 121.5 emergency frequency when you have nothing better to do.

Then get down to the nitty-gritty. Remove glasses unless you really can't see without them; even then, remove them just before touchdown. Discard pens and pencils from your shirt pockets. Remove dentures. Make certain the cabin latches are unlocked, particularly if the ship is pressurized. Some experts recommend opening the cabin door before landing and jamming it open with any handy item—flashlight, shoe, stack of maps, or whatever. Others feel that having an open door reduces the integrity of the cabin structure. Take your choice.

If there is a shoulder harness, use it. While half harness can cause twisting back injuries, they are much better than nothing. Seat belts and shoulder harness should be tight. If you have heavy objects loose in the cabin such as cameras, flashlights, ice chests, or water bottles, put them on the floor under the seats.

After that, you do the best you can with the equipment and the terrain you have to work with. Above all, keep your bird flying, not falling, just as long as you can—no slow and low steep turns; no stalling dirty at a hundred feet in the air.

Plan a touchdown at your slowest speed—uphill if the terrain permits. Keep the gear retracted in rough terrain. If you have power, land before your fuel is quite exhausted so a full "dead stick landing" will not be required. Then, just before touchdown, cut the switches and fuel off. After that it is purely academic.

After the dust has settled, get out of the cockpit. Count the number of passengers, if any, and get everyone away from the ship in case of post-crash fire (Fig. 11-2).

YOU'D BETTER TAKE IT WITH YOU

If you have a forced landing on a camping trip, you're better off than at any other time because your camping gear covers most of what you'll need for survival. However, most pilots carry a compact survival kit of some sort even on routine flights. We do.

A survival kit for your airplane is like its insurance policy: You buy it and hope you never need it.

Survival kits come in all shapes and sizes, ranging from the do-it-yourself package to a store-bought prefabricated selection that will contain hopefully all the goodies you may need regardless of where you go down. But you know full well that it ain't necessarily so.

Fig. 11-2. Kearsarge Pass, 11,898 feet MSL, in California's High Sierras has been the location of many lightplane crashes. This pass is on the direct flight route between Fresno, California and Las Vegas, Nevada. The bare hillsides above timberline provide probably the best forced landing area here.

On one extreme, there is a minimal package that can be stuffed into the barrel of a fountain pen or a penlight case. Insert matches and water purification tablets and seal it in wax. Add a magnetized needle for a compass, safety pins, a candle, thread, wire and foil. Hang the magnetized needle from the thread to find a northerly heading, assuming that the aircraft compass is not available. The aluminum foil can be shaped around the piece of wire to make a water utensil of sorts. Your mini-knife can be a single-edged injector razor blade. This package is not really uptown, but it is a start.

The size of your aircraft may influence your selection. Small single-seat homebuilts and ultralights can cram many of the essentials into a 4 1/2" × 6 1/2" × 1 3/4" metal container that will be waterproof when taped and later available to heat water in or even use as a digging tool. Such a tiny container can carry a Boy Scout or Swiss Army knife, candles, waterproof matches, signal mirror, single-edge razor blade, strong string or light rope, water purification tablets, ziplock bags for storage or water purification, sugar cubes or hard candy in sealed containers, tape, whistle, fishhooks and line, and needle and thread.

For aircraft that travel farther afield, add more tools, shelter material, insect repellent, food, and a first aid kit.

Personal medications as such usually go in your carry-on overnight bag. However, anyone with a critical problem (i.e., insulin for diabetic family members) might want to carry a limited supplemental supply in the survival kit. If you have the need, you might throw in an extra pair of prescription glasses.

DO-IT-YOURSELF SURVIVAL KITS

Cliff Springberg, for many years an equipment mechanic for the FAA in Alaska, had what was a novel way of outfitting his plane for survival: "An outdoor man doesn't really need too much—a box of matches, some salt, a rifle, ammo, and a fishing pole. After that, he can start adding items." One item that he considered as a standard was a five-gallon can of dry food—rice, beans, noodles and the like—all mixed together! "If I'm ever forced down, there'll be plenty of time to sort them out," he explained. (Before coming to Alaska, Springberg was a circus performer in the Lower 48. His circus act included a dive into a tank of water from a platform 110 feet up.)

The do-it-yourself survival kit can range from impulse buying at the local supermarket and drygoods stores to an expensive visit to the neighborhood backpacking outlet. Of course, anything you carry is somewhat better than nothing.

If you plan to outfit your own survival kit, consider using a list from an established survival manual as a starting point and then adapt it to the size of your airplane and the areas over which you normally fly. No survival kit, no matter how extensive, will work in all climates with any sort of efficiency. Most experts recommend including a survival information booklet that is designed to help focus the mind to constructive action and reduce panic.

We've been guilty for years of carrying a few of the most basic requirements in an old canvas suitcase that does double duty as a minimal tool kit for the most basic field maintenance—things like wooden matches in a sealed 35mm film container, a signaling mirror, a couple of lightweight Mylar wind and rain tarps, perhaps a granola bar or two, a hunting knife, and a short-handled axe that doubled as a sledge to drive in aluminim extrusions for tiedowns.

PACKAGED SURVIVAL KITS

At a midwest fly-in (Oshkosh), we happened to sit in on a survival clinic given by C. Bart and Dianne Whitehouse of Littleton, Colorado. He had some different ideas than those of the old school of survival, where you learned to live off the land on bugs and berries. His approach centered around a compact, complete kit in backpack form that could be pulled out of the airplane as you leave it.

Whitehouse has packaged his version of a survival package, called Res-Q-Pak, for two people; it weighs just eight pounds. The larger pack for four to six people is double that weight. These prefabricated kits have a number of advantages. They are assembled by experts in the field after extensive testing in the back country. The list of items is studied carefully for a cost/weight/size effectiveness. Edibles are protected for long shelf life quality. Basic tools, lights, and other essentials are included. The economy package is $150 (in 1984 dollars) for the two-person unit (Fig. 11-3).

Design of the Res-Q-Pak is straightforward. Whitehouse wanted to put a small, lightweight package containing the bare necessities within easy reach so that an exiting pilot could pick it up on his way out of the cockpit. He felt that bulkier, heavier survival packages would probably be carried on the floor of the baggage compartment, where they would stand a chance of being con-

Fig. 11-3. Dianne and Bart Whitehouse hold their small Res-Q-Pak. The prepared survival pack has shoulder straps for backpack carrying.

sumed by a post-crash fire. The main danger immediately following a crash landing is fire, usually from fuel spilling on hot engine parts. In most cases, the fire will start in the engine compartment, so there should be enough time for crew members to exit, grabbing the handy Res-Q-Pak on the way out.

Each Res-Q-Pak contains the basics—a tent, blankets, wind/rain pullovers, firemaking material, signals, including serial flares, smoke bomb and mirror. A strobelite is provided with the more expensive units. There are water containers and purification tablets, a first aid kit, basic food rations for two to three days with cooking cup and tools, including a spiral saw, knife, compass, chemical light, and rope (Fig. 11-4).

Whitehouse pointed out that there has been a change in philosophy about survival and the equipment to make it work. If you can remember back to WWII (and Whitehouse can), the survival manuals taught us how to live off the food on the land. They forgot to point out that a body needs only a very small amount of food to remain in good health for several days.

"Remember the instructions showing how to build a desert still in the summer. The statistics I've seen indicate that you'll perspire out more water in digging the hole than you'll get back in a reasonable time," Whitehouse said. "Many older kits stressed the

132

need for an ax. In my opinion, an ax or any other bludgeon-type tool is the last thing you want. In the first place, an ax is dangerous in the hands of a novice and another gash in a leg is something you don't need. You want a machete or a non-folding knife with a big handle. For cutting wood or clearing a path, carry a folding pull saw; a pruning saw is excellent.''

When it comes to lighting, Whitehouse feels that a chemical light is a good backup to a flashlight. He cites the American Cyanamid as being superior. The unit was developed for the U.S. Navy for a non-battery, non-heat, non-sparking light source that could be used in an explosive atmosphere. He reported that the design scientists went back to study lightning bugs in development of this product.

In actual "saves" with Whitehouse's packs, the plastic police whistle has proven invaluable in leading rescuers to the survivors when the search narrows down to an area where you're too close to the ELT. Plastic rather than metal whistles are recommended because extremely cold weather can cause metal to stick to the lips.

Fig. 11-4. Here's what's inside the Whitehouse Res-Q-Pak. All items in this package have been analyzed carefully by survival experts and are considered to be the most useful items. Such a pack should be carried in a cross-country lightplane at all times, not just when you plan to go air camping.

Crash survival statistics from the Air Force Rescue Coordination Center show that only about 35 out of 100 occupants will survive; 21 of the 35 will be injured and after 24 hours, only 7 of the 35 will still be alive. Survival percentage should be better in the general aviation field, where touchdown speeds are slower. However, whatever crash pack you carry, be it a paper bag from the supermarket or your own choice of ingredients and materials, that's what you are going to have to work with to stay alive in some semblance of comfort until help arrives.

WITHOUT WATER YOU'RE IN A DRY STATE

Water is the key to survival. The hotter and the drier the terrain, the sooner you'll need water. If you make a forced landing in arid terrain, you have a serious problem unless you have carried water with you.

Among our travels, we visited Australia and took the time to get a U.S. Pilot's Certificate validated there so we could cruise around that vast country on our own. Our check pilot was Des O'Driscoll, who works out of Southern Aircraft, Parafield Aerodrome, Adelaide, South Australia (Mailing address: P.O. Box 101, Pinnaroo, South Australia 5304). He is available to check out foreign pilots and also help them with the written exam. At the time we visited, Australia was suffering a severe drought and Adelaide broke a 20-year temperature record the day we were learning Australia's air traffic system with O'Driscoll in his 150-hp Cherokee. This was at a time when TAA, the Australian airline, was promoting a summertime tour to "See Alice When It's Hot!" "Alice" is Alice Springs in the center of the outback, and O'Driscoll commented that this was a trip not recommended for light aircraft before the month of April. "It's a question of safety and density altitude," explained the Australian flight instructor. "This time of the year, I carry four gallons of water in the back of my aircraft even if I'm going to stay in the local flying area."

The practicality of a desert still is open to question. Survival expert C. Bart Whitehouse, as mentioned previously in this chapter, feels that stills are counter productive and not worth the physical effort. However, many saves have been attributed in the past to these stills, and we would be remiss in not including a sketch of a desert still and a few details on how to build one (Fig. 11-5).

A water still made out of any can and a sheet of clear plastic will produce up to three pints of water a day out of hot desert sands. The still is made by digging a hole, placing a can or other container

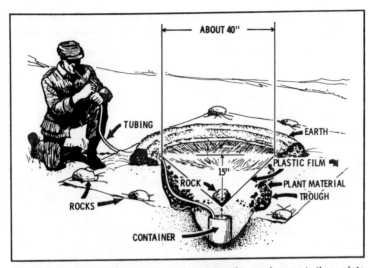

Fig. 11-5. Desert still, illustrated here, is supposed to produce up to three pints of water per day. Use of a tube to withdraw water makes it unnecessary to disturb the still. Thus, add a length of small plastic hose to your survival kit.

in the bottom, and covering the hole with a sheet of plastic.

The center of the plastic is pushed down to form a cone over the can. As air under the plastic gets hot, moisture from the ground evaporates to condense on the underside of plastic, and the drops running down the plastic will collect in the container.

A tube is inserted in the can and run to the surface to enable drinking from the container without disturbing the still.

However, obtaining water is only half the battle. You must make it last by conserving perspiration. The body gets rid of heat through evaporation or perspiration. As the body fluids drop, perspiration is reduced. An increase of six degrees from normal temperature is fatal. Although it may feel cooler with your clothes off, you are losing body fluids rapidly. Being fully clothed keeps the heat out and slows evaporation. The main points to remember are to drink water and preserve perspiration to avoid dehydrating.

In hot deserts you need a minimum of a gallon of water a day (Table 11-1). If you walk in the cool desert night you can get approximately 20 miles for that daily gallon. If you travel in daytime heat, you'll be lucky to get 10 miles to the gallon.

STAY WITH YOUR DOWNED PLANE

Unless there are compelling reasons to do otherwise, stay with

Table 11-1. Daily Water Requirements to Maintain Water Balance.

Mean Temperature Degrees F	Pints per 24 Hours
95	9
90	6 1/2
85	4 1/2
80	2 1/2
75	2

the aircraft you just crashed as it will have many of the luxuries that will help keep you alive. The airframe, or what's left of it, provides shelter and fuel can help start a fire if handled properly. Oil, tires, and a little fuel will generate a black signal smoke. Wiring cables and seat belts will double as rope for a lean-to shelter, building a stretcher, or whatever. Don't forget the compass in the wreck, just in case your homebuilt survival kit doesn't have one, if you decide to leave the vicinity of the unplanned landing.

While you're contemplating your future after that successful forced landing, look back through your charts for the Flight Service Station enroute frequencies. If you have an operating two-way radio, monitor that frequency until you hear a high-flying jet call in. Then get on the air and tell your troubles to the crew (Fig. 11-6).

Fig. 11-6. Rugged terrain like this can make rescue difficult. ELT signals can be blanked out by rock walls in some directions. A flight plan is always added insurance in sparsely populated areas.

Remember that the accepted international distress code includes three signal fires—the smokier the better—set in a triangle at least 20 yards apart. Then, when you hear a search aircraft, light up.

RODENTS TRY TO SURVIVE, TOO

The soft-pack container has a number of advantages in that it will stow easily under a seat and can be carried on the back with little effort. However, there can be at least one disadvantage with the cloth container, and we had it happen to us a number of years ago. Our Cessna 170B had space around the tailwheel where small animals such as rats could climb up inside the fuselage. We prepared for a trip one day and found that some enterprising rodent had devoured most of the munchies in our crash bag. However, if your airplane has relatively tight door seals and no open spots under the belly of the beast or around a tailwheel, this should not occur—but is worth the exercise to pull that pack out occasionally just to make certain that it's all there.

Another supplier of prefabricated kits is Survival 6-Pak. Their six-pound package lists for $99.95 plus $3.50 for shipping. This company has a unique guarantee that states, "If the Survival 6-Pak is ever used in an actual survival or life-saving situation, upon presentation of documented proof (i.e., newspaper clippings) and a letter from the user explaining the situation that required the use of the survival kit, you will be refunded the original purchase price and replacement of the unit at no cost." However, Survival 6-Pak adds, "Getting hungry on a long cross-country flight and snitching a Hershey bar from the Food Pak does *not* constitute a survival situation."

SOMETHING NEW FOR EVERYONE

Bob Jones, former Army radioman and private pilot, has hiked to the top of 14,495-foot Mt. Whitney seven times and is a High Sierra guide for Southern California scout troops. He has a number of survival ideas we had not heard of before. For example, he carries fishing gear and other small items inside the aluminum tubes of his backpack frame. He puts his clothing (one change only and two extra pairs of socks) in the bottom third of his backpack, where it will stay the driest. Then come his cooking utensils with food, and finally tent and ground tarp. He uses a small tube tent as a ground cover for his main tent and thus has a spare just in case.

In a small emergency pack that he feels is good for three days in the wilds, he has small amounts of concentrated food and grain in plastic prescription bottles. This wheat grain can be chewed without water. Liquid soap is carried the same way. He carries a whistle and tape as well as paper towel sections that have been soaked in hot wax and then rolled tightly in a small packet for quick fire starting. There are pieces of aluminum foil that can be unrolled as the "catcher" for a desert sill. He has nylon rope, an X-Acto blade or two, compass, first aid kit, and sewing kit. He carries two small pan warmers with a single charcoal stick inside each. These units were originally designed for elderly rest home residents to apply localized heat for aching areas. Jones uses them to keep feet and hands warm at night. He carries a lightweight windbreaker jacket with a hooded coller and a quart can of water.

On lower altitude trips where he can handle the extra weight, he takes a two-meter Kentwood TR25 transceiver, which sells for about $500 and will handle messages from many remote mountainous areas via relays that have been installed by ham radio operators. (Jones is WA6ZVJ.)

REQUIRED SURVIVAL PACKAGES IN THE FAR NORTH

Survival equipment is not only good sense when flying over isolated terrain. It is also a legal requirement in many parts of the world. In Canada and Alaska, for example, you are required to carry the following survival equipment—a package that is designed specifically for the wastelands of the far north. Actually, you will find that much of this required material is already in your camping gear:

Emergency Equipment for Flights in Canada

- ☐ Food having a calorific value of at least 10,000 calories per person carried, cannot be subject to deterioration by heat or cold, and must be stored in a sealed waterproof container bearing a tag or label on which the operator of the aircraft or his representative has certified the amount and satisfactory condition of the food in the container following an inspection made not more than six months prior to the flight.
- ☐ Cooking utensils.
- ☐ Matches in waterproof container.
- ☐ A stove and a supply of fuel or a self-contained means of

providing heat for cooking when you are operating north of the tree line.
- [ ] A portable compass.
- [ ] An ax of at least 2 1/2 pounds or 1 kilogram weight with a handle of not less than 28 inches or 70 centimeters in length.
- [ ] A flexible saw blade or equivalent cutting tool.
- [ ] Snare wire of at least 30 feet or 9 meters and instructions for its use.
- [ ] Fishing equipment including still-fishing bait and a gill net of not more than a 2-inch or 5-centimeter mesh.
- [ ] Mosquito nets or netting and insect repellent sufficient to meet the needs of all persons carried when operating in an area where insects are likely to be hazardous.
- [ ] Tents or engine and wing covers of suitable design, color or having panels colored in international orange or other high-visibility color, sufficient to accommodate all persons carried when operating north of the tree line.
- [ ] Winter sleeping bags sufficient in quantity to accommodate all persons carried when operating in an area where the mean daily temperature is likely to be 7 degrees C or less.
- [ ] Two paris of snowshoes when operating in areas where the ground snow cover is likely to be 12 inches or 30 centimeters or more.
- [ ] A signalling mirror.
- [ ] At least three pyrotechnical distress signals.
- [ ] A sharp jack knife or hunting knife of good quality.
- [ ] A suitable survival instruction manual.
- [ ] Conspicuity panel.

Emergency Equipment for Flights in Alaska

Alaska law requires the following minimum items for cross-country flying during the summer months.

- [ ] Emergency locator beacon.
- [ ] Food for each occupant sufficient to sustain life for two weeks.
- [ ] One axe or hatchet.
- [ ] One first aid kit.
- [ ] One pistol, revolver, shotgun or rifle and ammunition for same.

- ☐ One small fishnet and an assortment of tackle, such as hooks, flies, lines, sinkers, etc.
- ☐ One knife.
- ☐ Two small boxes of matches.
- ☐ One mosquito headnet for each occupant.
- ☐ Two small signaling devices, such as colored smoke bombs, railroad fuses, or Very pistol shells in sealed metal containers.

The following additional (minimum) items are required from October 15 to April 1.

- ☐ One pair of snowshoes.
- ☐ One sleeping bag.
- ☐ One wool blanket for each occupant over four years of age.

Note that a survival manual is required in emergency kits. Experts explain the need for such a publication as a checklist for pilots suffering some manner of shock following an emergency landing. The U.S. Air Force has an excellent S&R manual that is normally available on request. The RCAF has a number of booklets. One publication, *Survival Hints for the Sportsman,* includes the following about insects—something you can almost depend on following a forced landing.

"Insects. The ferocity and persistence of insects in the bush are always an unpleasant surprise, even to those previously warned against them. The black flies can be most troublesome and short exposure to them can make life unbearable.

"There are three methods of protection from insects available to you. None of them affords complete protection, but they reduce the discomfort considerably.

"Make a smudge fire. Any green wood or green leaves will produce an insect-repellent smoke.

"Wrap handkerchief around neck and back of head, Arab-style, tucking well into shirt collar and hat. Tie clothing at wrists and tuck pants inside boots or socks.

"Insect repellent. Apply to the exposed skin every three hours."

BACK COUNTRY PRECAUTIONS

Whether it be in an air camping situation or one that has suddenly changed into pure survival, there are a number of useful tidbits of information found deep in the Forest Service informational booklets. The following are some of the suggestions they have regarding snakes and poison oak.

Rattlesnakes occur throughout the mountains and are easy to recognize by their triangular shaped heads and narrow necks.

Watch where you step and where you place your hands when hiking. Since rattlesnakes can't regulate their body temperature, they generally seek cool, shady places such as rock crevices or shadows during the heat of the day. After the sun goes down, they like to stretch out on the pavement to absorb the remaining heat.

Rattlesnakes avoid people if at all possible. If you do see one, give it a wide berth.

Poison oak is common in many areas. Learn to recognize it by its three-lobed leaves. The leaves can be dark or light green, yellow, red, or brown, depending on the time of year.

If you do come in contact with this plant, wash skin immediately with mild soap and water. Wash contaminated clothing when you get home.

IN CASE OF INJURY IN THE BACK COUNTRY

Prevention is the best first aid. It is desirable for parties to have adequate first aid knowledge and equipment to help themselves. Self-reliance is the key in the back country.

Injury in remote areas can be the beginning of a real emergency. Stop immediately! Treat the injury if you can and make the victim comfortable. Send or signal for help. Three of anything is the international call for help—for example, three shots, three shouts, or three columns of smoke. If you must go for help, leave one person with the injured. If rescue is delayed, make an emergency shelter. Don't move until help arrives unless there is more danger in remaining where you are; use extreme care in moving the injured.

HYPOTHERMIA: THE NUMBER ONE KILLER

Be aware of the danger of hypothermia—subnormal temperature of the body. Lowering internal temperature may lead to mental and physical collapse and death. Hypothermia is caused by combinations of cold, wetness, and wind and is aggravated by exhaustion. It is the Number One killer of outdoor recreationists.

Cold kills in two distinct steps. The first step is exposure and exhaustion. The moment you begin to lose heat faster than your body produces it, you are undergoing exposure. Two things happen: You voluntarily exercise to stay warm, and your body makes involuntary adjustments to preserve normal temperature in the vital organs. Both responses drain your energy reserves. The only way to stop the drain is to reduce the degree of exposure.

The second step is hypothermia. If exposure continues until your energy reserves are exhausted, cold reaches the brain, depriving you of judgement and reasoning power. *You will not be aware of this happening.* You will lose control of your hands. This is hypothermia. Your internal temperature is sliding downward. Without treatment, this slide leads to stupor, collapse, and death.

The defense against hypothermia is to stay dry. When clothes get wet, they lose about 90 percent of their insulating value. Wool loses less heat than cotton, down, and some synthetics.

The victim may deny any problem. Believe the symptoms, not the victim. Even mild symptoms demand immediate treatment. Get the victim out of the wind and rain. Strip off all wet clothes. If the victim is only mildly impaired, give warm drinks. Get the person into warm clothes and a warm sleeping bag. Well-wrapped, warm (not hot) rocks or canteens will help.

If the victim is badly impaired, attempt to keep him or her awake. Put the victim in a sleeping bag with another person—both stripped. If you have a double bag, put the victim between two warm people. Build a fire to warm the camp.

Table 11-2. Wind Chill Cooling Power of Wind Expressed as Equivalent Chill Temperature.

mph	Temperature (F)											
Calm	40	30	20	10	5	0	-10	-20	-30	-40	-50	-60
	Equivalent Chill Temperature											
5	35	25	15	5	0	-5	-15	-25	-35	-45	-55	-70
10	30	15	5	-10	-15	-20	-35	-45	-60	-70	-80	-95
15	25	10	-5	-20	-25	-30	-45	-60	-70	-85	-100	-110
20	20	5	-10	-25	-30	-35	-50	-65	-80	-95	-110	-120
25	15	0	-15	-30	-35	-45	-60	-75	-90	-105	-120	-135
30	10	0	-20	-30	-40	-50	-65	-80	-95	-110	-125	-140
35	10	-5	-20	-35	-40	-50	-65	-80	-100	-115	-130	-145
40	10	-5	-20	-35	-45	-55	-70	-85	-100	-115	-130	-150
Danger				Increasing Danger (Flesh may freeze within 1 min.)				Great Danger (Flesh may freeze within 30 seconds)			

Fig. 11-7. Black bears inhabit the forested areas throughout the United States. All bears are dangerous animals and their behavior is unpredictable.

Wind, temperature, and moisture are factors that can greatly affect the safety of a backpacker. Each contributes to the loss of body heat. The wind chill chart illustrates the effect of wind and temperatures on dry, exposed flesh (Table 11-2).

BEAR BRIEFING FROM THE FOREST SERVICE

Grizzly bears live in Yellowstone and Glacier National Parks and portions of the surrounding forests in Montana, Wyoming, and Idaho. Black bears inhabit the forested areas throughout the United States (Fig. 11-7). Alaskan brown bears and grizzly bears are extremely dangerous. They exploit whatever opportunities they have for food sources.

All bears are dangerous animals. They are usually secretive creatures and stay away from people. But, if you are in bear country, be on the alert and take precautions. Remember, there are no hard and fast rules to ensure protection from a bear. Bear behavior differs under different conditions (Fig. 11-8).

Bears don't like surprises. Traveling alone in grizzly bear country is not recommended. When in grizzly bear country, make your presence known. Many experienced hikers wear bells, dangle a can of rattling pebbles, whistle, talk loudly, or sing—although noise is not a foolproof way to deter bears.

A surprise encounter, particularly with a female bear and cubs, is dangerous. A normally placid mother may be quickly provoked if her cubs are disturbed or if you come between her and her cubs. If you see a bear, give it plenty of room. Do not make abrupt moves or noises that would startle the bear. Slowly detour, keeping upwind so it will get your scent and know you are there. If you can't detour, wait until the bear moves away from your route.

Odors attract bears. The Forest Service offers the following suggestions to keep odors at a minimum:

Pack out all garbage in sealed containers. Make sure items such as empty food containers are clean and odor-free. When camping, it is best to use freeze-dried food instead of fresh food. Store food in plastic bags out of reach of bears and well away from sleeping areas. Sleep some distance from your cooking area. Don't sleep in the same clothes you wore when cooking.

Cook with gasoline or liquid petroleum burners instead of making campfires. Don't use perfumes, deodorants, or other sweet-smelling substances. Personal cleanliness is good insurance. Menstruation odors attract bears. Women should stay out of bear country during their menstrual periods. Human sexual activity attracts bears.

And with these words of caution from the Forest Service, let's leave the bears to their own devices and head for home.

SATELLITES TO THE RESCUE

The advent of worldwide satellite monitoring has changed the entire face of crash survival. Now somebody is really listening for you. Your operative ELT will almost always show up on the satellite with an immediate relay to ground stations, pinpointing the exact location of the signal.

Now when you pack a survival package, you can be fairly well assured that you won't be down and forgotten.

However, just as important for flights into rugged terrain is some sort of a flight plan, whether it be a formal FAA flight plan or just a preflight notification to a knowledgeable friend of where you're going, by which route, and when you expect to return.

Ken Burton of Stark Survival Training, Panama City, Florida, states that it takes 13 hours on an average to locate a downed aircraft that was on an IFR flight plan. It will take an average of 37 hours to reach a crash site if a VFR flight plan has been filed. Burton notes, "No flight plan—100 hours plus. The arrival of help may be hours after sighting."

Carrying some sort of a survival kit is just good insurance. As aircraft equipment becomes increasingly dependable and navcoms more a way of life, the chances of using your survival package becomes somewhat more remote. But wouldn't you feel oh-so-foolish to make an unscheduled landing out in the boonies and not be able to build even a signal fire? But, of course . . . it'll never happen to *you*!

Chapter 12

On Returning Home

Taking things in chronological order, we'd hope that you return from your first camping soiree all relaxed, tanned, maybe mosquito-bitten, and full of new stories to tell. If you enjoyed that first trip—and you should—it's already time to think about it all over again. If you're already an old hat at this business, add another notch to your tent pole and look ahead to next time.

Winding up your trip properly can be almost as important as the initial planning (Fig. 12-1). If you disassemble your gear in some logical order, you'll find it so much easier to launch next time. Unpack the plane and put it back in a people-packing configuration. Fill the oxygen bottle, if required; put in the back seat; change the oil, if required; bring your maintenance up to date and do the paperwork on the logs, both aircraft and personal. You'll be surprised how frequently you check back into those personal logbooks to find the name of an airport, the flight distance from one spot to another, or review whatever comments you might make.

For example, under Costerisan Farms in California, where we fly into and camp on occasion to cover ultralight activities, the comment could read, "Pet geese wander through camping areas; they're noisy at night."

Put your charts in order and pack the distant ones away until your next trip. And be sure to turn off the master switch!

If you're lucky enough to have a hangar (Fig. 12-2), you won't have to wrestle your camping gear in and out of your car. Every

Fig. 12-1. Imagine the work to unpack all this camping gear once this Piper arrives back home. The Pacer is shown in camping area at Oshkosh. If organized properly, it will all work smoothly.

time we fill a full-sized car with camping gear, cameras, clothes, and all that good stuff, we wonder how it fit in the plane. But it did.

Most pilots will have to haul all that gear home. Check your tent, sleeping bags, and other cloth items to assure that they are completely dry before you pack them away. Mildew generates a long-lasting, hard-to-get-rid-of odor and the presence of water in the cloth as it is packed away can cause deterioration.

If you have taken out any special trip insurance on your plane, don't forget to notify your agent and have it cancelled. This is particularly true on Mexican flights, where a special Mexican public liability policy is required while flying in that country.

If you've borrowed something for the trip—and don't we all— be sure to take it back to the lender. You may need it again.

Check your foodstuffs and put any partially used items back

Fig. 12-2. All this camping gear, including the Honda, fits nicely in a corner of the Binnall's hangar at Cable Airport.

on your pantry shelf. Mark your batteries and propane bottles with the amount of time they have been used so you won't wind up at the start of your next wilderness experience packing session wondering whether or not to buy any more. Normally, pressure containers of this type that have been opened once will have a tendency to dissipate on the shelf, so best buy at least one new unit just to be sure.

MORE PAPERWORK

Remember that daily diary that was recommended. During a quiet evening, go through it and relive the trip (Fig. 12-3). Extract the notes of things you wished you had on a list for next time. Write down the names of the people you met and those with whom you want to exchange correspondence or phone calls. See if there are "thank-you notes" to write.

Make up an accounting from gas receipts, meals (heaven forbid that you have a motel receipt except perhaps for every fourth night). Don't forget the cost of the charts, the phone calls, the mileage on your car in getting errands done before flight, film and processing—all those things that you would not have done if you hadn't gone air camping. You may want to keep the total strictly to yourself, or within the family, but it will give you an idea of how far you can go next time without busting a budget.

MEMORIES ON FILM

Get your precious color film to a good lab for processing. We

Fig. 12-3. One of the weird things you might want to explain in a trip diary is this picture. Two llamas dubbed Orville and Wilbur live in a pasture adjoining the flight strip at Mackay Bar, Idaho. This is noteworthy.

Fig. 12-4. Beech Bonanza passes picturesque villages and palm trees just north of San Blas on the west coast of Mexico. This is a fine trip destination when it is snowy up north.

use Eastman for 35mm slides and Color House, a large commercial film processer in Burbank, California, for the larger 120 color film. If you are shooting color negative and receive prints, make certain to order enough prints for the other people involved. A couple of pictures mailed out to people who were helpful on your camping flight will make you—and those who follow you—just that much more welcome in the future.

After your film comes back, go through the slides as objectively as you can. "Deep six" the bad ones, separate the look-alikes, and retain only the best. Then put them in a logical order and offer to do a slide show with a question-and-answer session on air camping for your local pilot group. Don't forget to include a photo or two of your camping gear being tested in the backyard before your trip. (You did take them, didn't you?)

LET'S DO IT AGAIN

When it comes to planning your next trip, you'll be much better equipped and informed after your first effort. For a change of pace, look for a seaside area if you've gone to the mountains (Fig. 12-4). Go with the seasons and head south for the winter. Some of the Gulf Coast resort areas have fine camping facilities near the shore. And vice versa: If you're in a hot, humid summer, you'll be looking for high mountains, tall pine trees, and crystal clear lakes in the northwest or in Canada. Comes time for the leaves to change color in the northeast and your flying tent will be a great asset because regular accommodations may be at a severe premium during this short season.

Consider international destinations. Canada has always been a comfortable first-time-out-of-the-country-with-your-plane place to go. There are no language problems, the food and water are all good, and flight planning with the associated search and rescue capability makes it almost like stateside.

Because we are located in Southern California, we have flown extensively in Mexico. The Mexican Government Tourism Department is doing a conscientious job of making private aircraft welcome in Mexico. We fly there all the time and have never had a problem, if you discount one load of watered gas several years ago in Baja California (Fig. 12-5). On Mexican flights, don't depend on credit cards for fuel. At this writing, they have been discontinued for use at the fuel pumps at least on the Baja Peninsula. There are many excellent seaside areas, particularly on the West Coast of the mainland. Zihuatanejo, a hundred miles northwest of Acapulco, is one of the most picturesque places we've flown into. Once unspoiled, it is rapidly becoming a jet set hideaway, but there are a number of small airports (Fig. 12-6) up and down that section of the coast that look as though they would be worthwhile exploring.

Fig. 12-5. Adequate flight strip at Hotel Cabo San Lucas is located directly across the highway from this plush hotel at the tip of Baja California. Stop in for a Coke to see these expensive sights and then head on up the coastline for some isolated flight strip to enjoy the country on your own.

Fig. 12-6. Grassy parking area at San Blas on the west coast of Mexico would make an ideal spot for camping. Here a local resident will contract to watch your airplane for a few pesos while you walk or ride your Honda into town. Taxicabs are rare in San Blas.

The Bahamas have long been a popular destination for pilots and some air campers. That area is one mighty long flight from the West Coast and our contact in that areas has been limited to a couple of rental aircraft in the Caribbean, at St. Thomas and St. Croix in the Virgin Islands. The scenery is great and there are some fine airports.* However—and this is only our personal opinion— our single-engine aircraft immediately goes into automatic rough when we're out of gliding distance of land. On the 28-mile flight to Santa Catalina Island, for example, we'll have 10,000 feet at mid-channel. However, single-engine island hopping is a way of life to many people and we can't knock it.

We practice what we preach. As this book is being shipped to the publisher, our house is a minor shambles with a variety of small pasteboard packing boxes, sleeping bags, and tent, cameras and note pads. It's travel time again for us: First, the annual trek to Oshkosh; then on to Anchorage, Alaska, for a convention and a few days with friends. We'll visit new airports, see new people, and camp beside our Cardinal in some places we have never heard of—yet!

*See *Flying the Bahamas* by Frank Kingston Smith, TAB Book No. 2351, and *Your Mexican Flight Plan,* by Don & Julia Downie, TAB Book No. 2337.

Index

OTHER POPULAR TAB BOOKS OF INTEREST

TAB   TAB BOOKS Inc.

Blue Ridge Summit, Pa. 17214

Send for FREE TAB Catalog describing over 750 current titles in print.